Chuck Dougherty's
RUNNING WASHINGTON

A GUIDE TO 101 WASHINGTON AREA RUNNING TRAILS

VANDAMERE PRESS
a division of AB Associates

Published by
Vandamere Press
A division of AB Associates
P.O. Box 5243
Arlington, VA 22205

Copyright © 1984 by Vandamere Press

ISBN: 0-918339-01-4

Library of Congress Catalog Card Number
84-052351

Acknowledgements

In writing any book, there are always more people to thank than space available. A few people, however, must be mentioned. To my wife, Cynthia, who has been more than patient throughout this whole project, all I can say is thanks. Special credit also goes to my publisher, Art Brown of Vandamere Press, for pushing and harassing me to finish this project. Many thanks also to my editor, Pat Berger, for being very patient and thorough.

I would also like to thank Ms. Barbara Frech, President of the Northern Virginia Roadrunning Club, for her assistance in providing background on area running events.

Contents

Chapter 1
Introduction

Chapter 2
Downtown Sightseeing Trails

Chapter 3
Rock Creek Park

Chapter 4
Mount Vernon Trails

Chapter 5
The C&O Canal Overview

Chapter 6
Washington and Old Dominion Trail

Chapter 7
The District of Columbia

Chapter 8
Maryland

Chapter 9
Virginia

Chapter 10
Washington Area Running Events

Chapter 1
Introduction

Like most runners I began running for many reasons, but mostly to get my desk-bound body back into shape. I had no thoughts of exploring new places, running marathons, or writing a book. At first I ran the streets of my own neighborhood and felt a sense of real accomplishment when I began to run with less huffing and puffing. As my endurance grew, I began to develop enough courage and confidence to travel further and look for new places to run. I found that I enjoyed seeing Washington from sidewalks and trails rather than from a car window. I also began wondering where all the paths and trails went that I passed in my car or on the bus. Some trails followed freeways for miles and then disappeared into wooded sections. Others were only visible at their beginning or end. I began to wonder how many of these paths were runnable and where they went. It was the old question of "What's on the other side of the hill?". I looked in book stores for current maps or books which could provide lists and details of trails which were acceptable for running. When I found that none met my need, I began keeping notes on trails that I ran. Eventually, my publisher convinced me there were other runners who would find these notes interesting and useful. As a result, I began what was to become a 6-month ordeal of working and writing, unfortunately with only a minimal amount of time left for running.

Greater Washington is a very diverse area. There are long trails passing through the heart of the metropolitan area that can not only transport you to deep woods, but, in fact, allow you to run almost the entire area using the interconnected parkland. There are trails with steep hills and trails with long slopes. There are level flat trails that stretch out in front of you as if you were running on the Great Plains instead of in the nation's capitol. There are bogs and rivers to run along, with a wide variety of wildlife around them. I have seen beavers, possums, deer, fox, and all types of birds and waterfowl within 10 miles of the White House. There is, of course, one feature of Washington that cannot be duplicated in any other city—the monuments, historical sites, and places of national interest.

In this book, I will try to introduce you to all the various types of trails throughout the entire region. The trails have been grouped into eight chapters. Four of the chapters are based on major trail systems, each of which contains numerous individual running trails. Chapter 2 is provided for traveling professionals, tourists, and newcomers who want to see the sights and still get some exercise. The remaining three chapters contain a mixed bag of trails which cover the three "states" that comprise the Washington area.

The trails within each chapter are arranged in a rough geographical order. Each trail description begins with a *location* header to provide you with the general area of the trail within the "state" or park. This is followed by information on distance, surface, rating, and population. *Distance*, unless otherwise specified, refers to the round trip distance. Every attempt has been made to make these measurements as accurate as possible; however, due to the nature of the trails, measurements should not be considered to be exact. *Surface* refers to the most common surface or surfaces along the trail. Exceptions are noted in the trail write-up that follows. *Rating* refers to both the running difficulty and trail conditions. A number *1* is an excellent trail that will provide you with challenge and entertainment. A number *2* is an average trail, one that can be run with ease but will not provide an especially memorable experience. Number *2* trails are excellent for novice runners. A number *3* is generally more satisfactory for jogging than running. At times a *3* can be challenging just to find the trail. *Population* is rated on the same scale, *1*, to *3*. The number of people on a trail can vary based on the day of the week and the time of day. I have attempted to show the average number of people on each trail at any given time. A *1* is a high-density trail. A *2* has some people but is not overly crowded. Number *3* has very few runners, or anyone else, for that matter.

Each trail is also accompanied by a map to help you follow what may, at times, seem to be somewhat complex, written directions. Unless otherwise noted, all maps have been drawn to a scale of one mile for two and five-eights inches or one mile to one inch. North is indicated on each map with a large arrow. Smaller arrows indicate direction to run and points of interest. Interconnections with other trails are indicated with references to the crossing trails' page number.

At this point we should discuss safety. The one rule of safety that applies to all runners in all situations is "Never run alone." All other considerations are secondary. For Washington area runners there are three major areas of concern. First, all runners are aware of the normal medical dangers in running. Cuts, sprains, bites, and other minor injuries are part of running. Care and common sense can minimize your damages. More serious medical problems are not within the purview of this book, but suffice it to say, no one should run without a full physical examination and a doctor's approval. Second, Washington is a major urban center with the usual major urban center crowding. Never cross a street without looking both ways. While that may seem obvious to everyone over the age of four, runners get so involved in the "challenge" that they become oblivious to traffic around them, often with fatal consequences. Bicyclists and pedestrians can also be a danger, though not often fatal. Third, and most unfortunately, runners must be concerned with crime. The many law enforcement agencies throughout the area do a commendable job patrolling these trails. I have found officers mounted on horseback patrolling in sparsely populated surroundings. I have passed officers on foot and in cars in all jurisdictions. In many cases, however, you may be the only person for miles. The Washington area should not be run in most areas after dark. Rock Creek Park is one of the city's most popular trails, but when the sun goes down the woods can come alive". Along the C&O Canal in Georgetown, even though there are lights on the trail, "crazies" appear at times along the trail. The border area between Prince Georges County and Washington is dangerous at most times and police caution against running at night, running alone, or just not paying attention to your surroundings. In Virginia, there have been a series of "flasher" incidents along the Mount Vernon trail over the past few years.

With this gloomy but necessary note of caution you are now ready to proceed to the rest of this book and the trails themselves. I hope that you will have as much fun *Running Washington* as I have in preparing this book, and that you will be challenged to run new areas that you otherwise might have missed. Happy Trails.

Chapter 2
Downtown Sightseeing Trails

Most books on Washington will tell you that our nation's capital is one of the unique cities of the world. What they don't tell you is that it is also a great city for running. Washington has numerous neighborhoods typical of any large city, but the downtown area with its various monuments and historic sites makes Washington a special place for all of us. Remember, Washington can be as interesting to run in as it is to walk and sightsee. Because of this interest in the monuments, public buildings, Mall, and Georgetown, I have devoted this chapter to these sightseeing areas. Running past these monuments does not place you on outstanding running trails; in fact, much of this running is often on sidewalks. However, it is easy and simple running if you allow for the large number of cross-streets and people.

The monuments to our nation's leaders are well-known sights. The museums of the Smithsonian Institution along the Mall contain much that is interesting from American art, history, and technology. The East and West Wings of the National Gallery of Art contain some of the best permanent and transient collections of art in the world. The John F. Kennedy Center for the Performing Arts is known worldwide for its entertainment and cultural events. Georgetown contains unique architecture dating from its earlier colonial period along with modern office buildings, small shops, restaurants, and bars.

The majority of the sites which you will pass on your run are not appropriate to visit in running attire; however, you can get a good overview of spots of interest by running through these areas and noting the locations of those you wish to visit later. Traffic in the Washington area can be as heavy as any city in the country. Extreme care must be used when crossing streets, alleys, and driveways.

If you are a tourist or a newcomer, you may not want to limit yourself to these special runs. Trails in the Mt. Vernon and C&O Canal chapters also offer runs past and through areas of great national and historic interest. Connections to these and other trails are indicated on the maps accompanying each trail.

West Potomac — East Potomac Park

Location: D.C., south of the Lincoln Memorial
Distance: 5.5 or 6.75   **Rating**: 1
Surface: Sidewalk or grass   **Population**: Varies

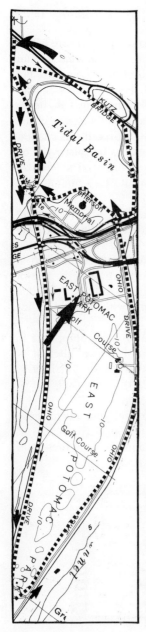

Park near the Lincoln Memorial on Ohio Drive. There are two choices available for running: one is to go south on the grass of the athletic fields next to the street; the other is to run south on the sidewalk next to the river. You will come to a small bridge between the Tidal Basin and the Potomac River. Run over this bridge and turn to the right. The bridge divides West Potomac and East .Potomac Parks. Continue running south under the two bridges that cross the river. Next, you will pass a public golf course in the middle of the park.

The "Awakening" statue at the end of the park is very interesting with arms and head extending up out of the ground. Pass the end of the park and run north along the Washington Channel. Next, run under the 14th Street Bridge approaches through a small tunnel. Cross the road that comes up to the Jefferson Memorial and the 14th Street Bridge. Be careful of the heavy traffic at this point. Continue to the Tidal Basin, turn to the left, and circle the bottom of the basin clockwise. This will take you past the Jefferson Memorial. Continue in the same direction, run along the approach road to the memorial, and over the same bridge that you crossed running south. Cut to the right and continue along the Tidal Basin on West Basin Drive. This is the area of the famous Japanese cherry trees. Another road will branch off to the left returning to Ohio Drive where you started. You can run the entire Tidal Basin, returning to the Jefferson Memorial. When running in the vicinity of the cherry trees, you can run on a path above the trees near the road or directly along the Tidal Basin. However, the numbers of people and low-hanging limbs of trees on the walkway next to the basin may be a problem.

Special Information: There are a number of water fountains in East Potomac Park and near the cherry trees. Also, there are comfort stations near Hains Point and in the vicinity of the cherry trees. In good weather there are more people milling around in East Potomac Park than probably any other area in Washington. However, when the weather is bad, this area is almost totally deserted. This can be a difficult run when cold winds blow off the Potomac River.

Lincoln Memorial — Kennedy Center — White House

Location: D.C., starting on the Potomac River
Distance: 3.2
Surface: Sidewalk, gravel

Rating: 1
Population: 1

Park near the Lincoln Memorial along the Rock Creek Parkway approach to the memorial or on Ohio Drive. Run north along Rock Creek Parkway from the Lincoln Memorial keeping the Potomac River on your left. Run down a slight grade from the memorial. On your right are a number of athletic fields where volleyball is quite popular on weekends during the warm months. Run under the Teddy Roosevelt Bridge and, once under the bridge, turn right crossing Rock Creek Parkway. Run up the grassy hill next to the bridge and across the approach road to the front of the Kennedy Center. Run three-quarters of the way along the front of the center. Make a right turn, cross the approach road, and follow a path that will bring you out on Virginia Avenue. Cross Virginia Avenue on G Street and continue on G Street until you reach 17th Street.

While running along G Street, you will pass George Washington University. At 17th Street, look to the right to see the Old Executive Office Building. Turn left and run to the corner of Pennsylvania Avenue. Crossing 17th Street, stay on the south side of Pennsylvania. Look for Blair House across the avenue. It is the guest house of the President. On the other side, you will be approaching the White House. Beyond the West Wing you will see a circular drive in the front. Note the cement walls erected for security along Pennsylvania Avenue. At the light, turn right on East Executive Drive which is closed to through traffic. You will be running between the Treasury Building and the East Wing of the White House. Near the light on the south end of the drive, cut across the road and run beside the White House fence. This is the best view of the White House. Next, cross Executive Drive and run along the road circling the Ellipse on the west side. On the southwest side of the Ellipse, follow the road that leads southwest to the corner of 17th Street and Constitution Avenue. Cross Constitution Avenue and turn right on the first path going into the Mall south of Constitution Avenue. Run past Constitution Gardens and the Vietnam Veterans Memorial, eventually returning to the Lincoln Memorial.
Special Information: Most of this run is over regular sidewalk. Water is available from fountains in the Mall. Running is not recommended after dark.

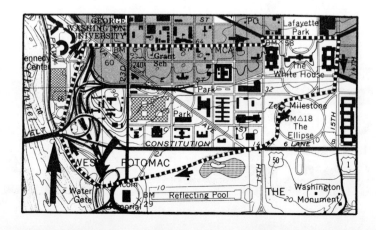

Mall — Capitol

Location: D.C., just south of the business district
Distance: 3.5
Surface: Gravel and sidewalk

Rating: 1
Population: 1

Start this trail at Metro's Smithsonian subway stop on the Mall. It is preferable to ride to this stop on Metro's blue or orange lines because parking is difficult in the Mall area. From the subway run east toward the Capitol. There are crushed stone paths that circle and cut across the Mall. All of the major museums and galleries ring the Mall. On the east side you will pass the Freer Gallery, Hirshhorn Museum, and Air and Space Museum, to name a few. Cross 3rd Street, Northwest, run around the Reflecting Pool, cut toward the Capitol, and turn north on 1st Street, Northwest. Cross Constitution Avenue and head toward the Taft Memorial Tower. Run back toward Constitution Avenue and continue east. The Senate Office Buildings are on the left side as you run east. Turn right on 1st Street and run past the Supreme Court and the Library of Congress. Turn right on Independence Avenue. The House Office Buildings will be on your left. On the Capitol side of the street, run down the hill on the access road in front of the Capitol. Run back toward the Mall along the north side of the Reflecting Pool. Cross 3rd Street and run the gravel path along the north side of the Mall. You will pass the East and West Wings of the National Gallery of Art and the Museum of History and Technology. At the museum, cross to the south side of the Mall and back to the subway stop where you began.

Special Information: Water fountains are available near all the museums and monuments. There is some shade near the sides of the Mall and around Capitol Hill. If you have never run the Mall, it is something you should do at least once. Be aware, however, that you may encounter large numbers of sightseers on the Mall.

Lincoln Memorial — Mall

Location: D.C., from the Potomac River, south of the White House and the business district

Distance: 4

Surface: Gravel, blacktop

Rating: 1

Population: 1

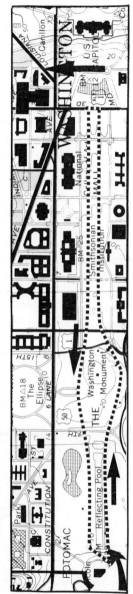

Park near the Lincoln Memorial on the Rock Creek Parkway approach from the north or on Ohio Drive located south of the memorial. Run around to the east side of the memorial which has steps leading up into the memorial. Run southeast from this point onto the path that goes east just south of the Reflecting Pool. This path has trees and benches along both sides. Cross 17th Street, cut south, and then run just north of the Independence Avenue extension. Cut to the left and run past the Washington Monument. Cross 15th Street, run up a small rise, and approach 14th Street. Run south and cross 14th Street near Jefferson Drive. Run toward the Capitol on the gravel path which is just to the north of Jefferson Drive. Enjoy the museums and galleries you will see on this part of the run. You will pass the Freer Gallery, the original Smithsonian Castle, the Hirshhorn Museum, and the Air and Space Museum. Run to the end of the gravel path and cut north along 3rd Street to just south of Madison Drive. Turn left on the gravel path, which runs just south of Madison Drive. While running past the East Wing of the National Gallery of Art, note the dark spot on the side of the building caused by the many people who have put their noses against the building to split their vision. Continue west past the National Gallery of Art, the Natural History Museum, and the Museum of History and Technology. Cross 14th Street and 15th Street, run north of the Washington Monument, and head for the Lincoln Memorial. Cross 17th Street and on the return trip stay to the north of the Reflecting Pool. When you reach the vicinity of the Lincoln Memorial, cool down and walk through the Vietnam Veterans Memorial. The extra time spent here is well worth the experience.

Special Information: Water fountains are available near all the museums and monuments. There is shade available. Remember that there will be many tourists and bicyclists on the Mall near the museums.

Lincoln Memorial — the Bridges — L.B.J. Park

Location: D.C. and Northern Virginia
Distance: 3.75 or 6.75   **Rating**: 1
Surface: Blacktop, sidewalk   **Population**: Varies, 2

   Park near the Lincoln Memorial on the Rock Creek Parkway approach or along
Ohio Drive. Run south along Ohio Drive. Cross the small bridge and run to the left
toward the Jefferson Memorial and then to the right toward the approach to the
14th Street Bridge. Take the walkway along the north side of the north span. When
you reach the other side, run to the right. Cross the Boundary Channel lagoon and
run the path behind the Navy and Marine Memorial to the first crosswalk on the
George Washington Parkway. Carefully, run across the parkway and into the L.B.J.
Park. There is a large stone monument there, dedicated to the memory of President
Johnson. Return to the parkway path and continue north on the path leading to
Memorial Bridge. Cross Memorial Bridge and return to your starting point or run
around the circle toward Arlington Cemetery. Cross to the north side of the road,
passing the Metro subway stop, the Seabee Memorial, and an exit ramp. Run down
the blacktopped trail along the exit ramp and then north along Arlington Cemetery.
Follow the path along the edge of the cemetery. Turn left and run west past two
small trees growing in the middle of the trail. Turn onto the road to your right.
Cross the street noting the Netherlands Carillons to the left. Continue on this road
which is an approach road for the Iwo Jima Memorial. Circle halfway around the
memorial to the northwest corner and run over a rise at the edge of the park
bringing you to the access ramps for Route 50. Cross the ramps using the
crosswalks and run north along the east side of North Fort Meyer Drive. Cross over
Route 50 and down a grade to Lynn Street leading you to an approach to Key
Bridge. Run across Key Bridge, staying on the east side, and turn right. Go one
block, turn right on 34th Street where you will find a ramp to the right to the C&O
Canal path. Run the C&O Canal path east when you reach the bottom of the ramp,
until you reach its junction with the Rock Creek Park path. Turn right on the Rock
Creek Park path. You will then run past the Watergate complex and the Kennedy
Center, arriving back at the Lincoln Memorial.

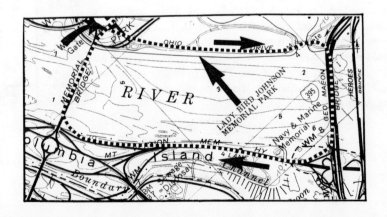

Lafayette Park — the Capitol — the Mall

Location: Northwest Washington in the heart of downtown Washington
Distance: 4
Surface: Sidewalk, gravel

Rating: 1
Population: 1

Start at Lafayette Park across from the front of the White House and just to the south of the hotels located at 16th and K Streets, N.W. Run to the southeast corner of Lafayette Park and notice the various statues in the park. Turn left on Pennsylvania Avenue and run in front of the Treasury Department. Pennsylvania Avenue makes a jog at the corner of the Treasury Building at 15th Street. Cross to the east side of the street and turn left on Pennsylvania Avenue which ends at the Capitol visible in the distance. At 12th Street and Pennsylvania Avenue is the Pavilion which contains many restaurants, shops, and the National Park Services's belltower. There is a glass-enclosed elevator to take you from the ground floor to the area of the bells and then another elevator to an open air view which I consider to be as good, if not better, than the view from the Washington Monument. From the Pavilion, continue running along Pennsylvania Avenue to the foot of the Capitol. Circle the Capitol clockwise returning to the bottom of the hill in front of the Capitol Reflecting Pool. Run around the Reflecting Pool and then west along the path by either Jefferson Drive or Madison Drive. There are many galleries and museums on both sides; these are described in other Mall run trails. Run up to the Washington Monument, then north through the parking lot of the monument, to Constitution Avenue. Cross Constitution Avenue, run along the east side of the Ellipse, cross E Street, and run north along East Executive Avenue which is closed to traffic. The Treasury Building will be on your right. Cross Pennsylvania Avenue to complete a large circle returning to your point of origin.

Special Information: There is a water fountain at the base of the Capitol. There are refreshments available at the Pavilion. There is shade at Lafayette Park and around the Capitol. This trail should not be run at night.

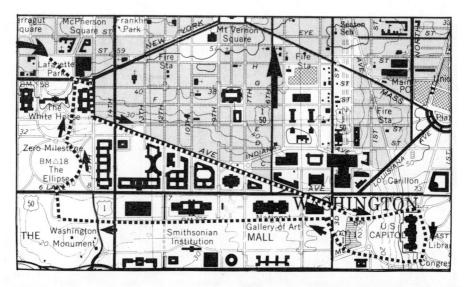

DuPont Circle — Scott Circle — Ellipse
Kennedy Center — Washington Hilton

Location: D.C., northwest of the White House
Distance: 3.5
Surface: Sidewalk

Rating: 2
Population: 1

Start this trail at DuPont Circle, one of the most cosmopolitan of neighborhoods within the District of Columbia. Run southeast along Massachusetts Avenue to 16th Street at Scott Circle, directly north of the White House. Scott Circle is lovely when the cherry trees are blossoming in early April. Turn south on 16th Street, run around the White House after passing through Lafayette Park, and run down East Executive Drive. Stay along the White House fence, running behind the White House and then behind the Old Executive Office Building. Run across 17th Street and then west on E Street for five blocks to Virginia Avenue. Turn right on Virginia Avenue and run north to G Street. Turn left at G Street and cross Virginia Avenue, coming out by the Watergate complex and the Kennedy Center. Turn right on New Hampshire Avenue and run northeast to Washington Circle. Head north on 23rd Street to Massachusetts Avenue and run northeast on Florida Avenue which joins 23rd Street at this point. This leg of Florida Avenue is a gently rising hill. Florida Avenue joins Connecticut Avenue at the Washington Hilton Hotel. To return to DuPont Circle, turn right on Connecticut Avenue and run back to your starting point.

Special Information: This running trail is on ordinary city streets in northwest Washington. The route suggested will take you through some interesting neighborhoods and will let you see some of Washington's interesting attractions. There is little shade available and no water fountains. As this trail primarily uses sidewalks, extreme care should be taken when crossing streets. This trail should not be run at night for safety reasons.

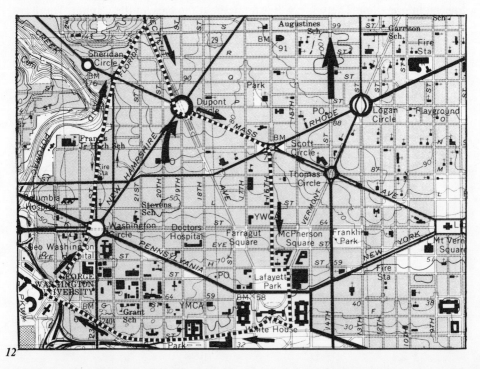

Georgetown — DuPont Circle
Lincoln Memorial — Kennedy Center

Location: Northwest District of Columbia near the Potomac River
Distance: 4.5   **Rating**: 2
Surface: Sidewalk, blacktop   **Population**: 1

Start at the bridge over Rock Creek Park at M Street, N.W. Run west on M Street. After passing 31st Street, you will come to Wisconsin Avenue, one of the principal streets through Georgetown. Turn right on Wisconsin Avenue and run north. This part of the trail will be generally uphill until you reach P Street. Turn right on P Street and run east through Georgetown coming out at DuPont Circle. Run southwest on New Hampshire Avenue to Washington Circle. Run across Washington Circle and then directly south on 23rd Street. This will bring you to the Lincoln Memorial. Run west along the north side of the Lincoln Memorial and then down the sidewalk along the Potomac River. This sidewalk will lead into the Rock Creek Trail. Continue north under the Roosevelt Bridge and you will see the Kennedy Center directly on your right. If you want to go to the front of the Kennedy Center, you must run up the grassy hill to the front of the center. Continue north on the Rock Creek Trail past Virginia Avenue and turn left as soon as you cross the little bridge that goes over the C&O Canal. This is the start of the C&O Canal Trail. Run west to the first cross-street which is 29th Street. Turn right and run north one block to come back to the vicinity of your starting point.

Special Information: The main streets of Georgetown cannot be run with ease at any time because of the number of people on the street. It is truly impossible to run on a weekend or when there is some special event. There is water available from a fountain located on the east side of the Lincoln Memorial. There are some shade trees located in the DuPont Circle area and in the vicinity of the Lincoln Memorial. This trail cannot be run at night as the lighting is insufficient.

Location: In the Potomac River, west of the Kennedy Center

Distance: 4.7   **Rating**: 1

Surface: Concrete, packed dirt   **Population**: 2

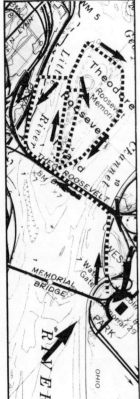

The best route to run to Theodore Roosevelt Island is along the north side of the Roosevelt Bridge. The approach for the north side of the bridge is located near the Kennedy Center. If you are running, the approach can be made by the Rock Creek Parkway Trail or the walkway in front of the Kennedy Center. From the parkway trail, cross the parkway to the east side as you approach the Roosevelt Bridge. Then run up onto the grass along the north side of the bridge approach. Turn right on the sidewalk that is the approach to the walk going over the bridge to the Virginia side. Upon leaving the bridge, locate a worn dirt path which you will take north through the grass along the George Washington Parkway. Continue along this path for a short distance to the parking lot for the island.

Cross the short concrete bridge that leads from the parking lot to the island. Run straight ahead onto a worn dirt path that will take you up a small hill, or turn to the right upon reaching the island. Both of these paths will exit at the open area surrounding the Teddy Roosevelt statue. If you like, run all the trails on the island; they are dirt or packed gravel. In early April, there may be high water in the Potomac River which may cause flooding of the Swamp Trail on the east side. This seems to be the case whenever the river is above its normal level. The run across the bridge is 1.1 miles, and there are 2.5 miles of path on the island itself.

Special Information: There are 88 acres on the island. It was dedicated in 1967 as a tribute to President Theodore Roosevelt who was at the forefront of the conservation movement in America in his day. The bronze statue of Roosevelt is 17 feet high and is surrounded by water-filled reflecting pools near the entrance close to the bridge. It is a lovely area and is not well known to most tourists or to residents in the Washington area. The island is open only during daylight hours. There is a gate on the footbridge crossing to the island which is closed at sundown. There are water fountains and a restroom on the island. If you wish to run just the island, you should travel south on the George Washington Parkway (Virginia) past the Memorial Bridge entrance. Look for the parking lot on the right.

Chapter 3
Rock Creek Park

Rock Creek Park is one of the most pleasurable spots in the Washington area. It stretches across various jurisdictions, starting in Washington, D.C. near the Potomac River and ending in Montgomery County, Maryland, northwest of the city. In Washington, Rock Creek Park is maintained by the National Park Service; in Maryland, it is under the control of the Maryland National Capital Park and Planning Commission. The Potomac Appalachian Trail Club also maintains trails within the park.

Beginning in the south at the Lincoln Memorial, Rock Creek Park is narrow but it widens considerably as it stretches north of the beltway in the vicinity of Lake Needmore in Montgomery County. There are numerous places where you can park, both in Montgomery County and within the District of Columbia. There are many picnic tables and water fountains throughout the park system.

Rock Creek Park also contains some interesting sights. For example, Pierce Mill, located near Tilden Street on the Rock Creek Trail, is a restored gristmill that is in actual operation between 9 a.m. and 5 p.m., Wednesday through Sunday. The Art Barn, located next to Pierce Mill, is a place where local artists display their work. South of the Art Barn and Pierce Mill and north of Cathedral Avenue is the National Zoological Park, one of the best zoos in the country.

The trails in the Rock Creek Park system are some of the best in the area. There are opportunities to run on almost all kinds of surfaces, paved asphalt, roadways blocked on the weekend, and crushed gravel or packed earth. Because of their popularity, you will find large numbers of runners, as well as bicyclists, using the trails in the lower portion of Rock Creek Park. As you go further north, however, the numbers decrease. A word of caution: Rock Creek Park should be avoided at night as lighting is nonexistent.

Overall, Rock Creek Park is a beautiful park with a gently running stream and hills covered by deep woods. For a really enjoyable experience, run the trails in the park. You will find them ideal. Remember, Rock Creek Park should not be run at night.

Lincoln Memorial — P Street

Location: Northwest Washington, D.C., near Georgetown
Distance: 3.3   **Rating**: 1
Surface: Blacktop   **Population**: 2

Park near the Lincoln Memorial on Ohio Drive to the south of the memorial or to the north along Rock Creek Drive. Run north along Rock Creek Drive down the hill from the memorial, under the Theodore Roosevelt Bridge, and past the Kennedy Center. In this part of the trail, you will be directly next to the Potomac River.

After passing the Kennedy Center, run past the Watergate complex on your right. Run under the Whitehurst Freeway extension. You will soon see the Four Seasons Hotel, located in Georgetown on your left and the start of the C&O Canal Trail. Run along the base of a hill curving gently to the right and then quickly to the left. At P Street, turn to the left, run up a steep hill, and follow the trail on top of the hill, which follows the Rock Creek Trail down below. The trail then emerges on M Street. Cross M Street and pass behind the Four Seasons Hotel to the C&O Canal Trail. Turn left on the C&O Canal Trail and run to the merger with the Rock Creek Trail. Run the Rock Creek Trail to the right back to your point of origin.

Special Information: Lower Rock Creek Park is the one part of the trail where you will see a number of famous Washington buildings. North of Virginia Avenue you will be in the woods. Watch out for the numerous bicyclists on the lower part of this trail, as the path is narrow and right next to the parkway. When you are on P Street, look across the parkway to see Georgetown's "P Street Beach," actually a large meadow. The Rock Creek Park trails should not be run in the evening.

Location: Northwest Washington, D.C., in Rock Creek Park

Distance: 4.5   **Rating**: 1

Surface: Blacktop   **Population**: 2

Park near Rock Creek Park at the P Street exit from the parkway at the edge of Georgetown. Run down the hill at the P Street exit ramp. When you reach the parkway, turn north on the park trail running along the west side of Rock Creek Park through the woods. After crossing a small bridge, you will once again be in the vicinity of the parkway.

Continue to run the trail along the parkway. You will pass through a course of exercise stations which are well-spaced and maintained. The start of the course is on the north end of Cathedral Avenue at the top of a small hill. The trail crosses the entrance to Rock Creek Park at Cathedral Avenue and goes down a small hill and under the Calvert Avenue Bridge. Cross Rock Creek, turn left just before the tunnel, and follow the stream until you come to the zoo maintenance road. Turn left and enter the zoo. You will have a long uphill run to the main entrance of the zoo on Connecticut Avenue.

Special Information: There is a water fountain in the middle of the exercise station course along the edge of Rock Creek Park. There is room to run along the edge of the trail and considerable shade. This particular path is one of the most popular trails in Washington. It should not be run at night. The best way to return is over the same trail.

National Zoo — Tilden
Connecticut — Cathedral

Location: Northwèst Washington, D.C., just east of Connecticut Avenue in Rock Creek Park

Distance: 3.5   **Rating**: 2

Surface: Blacktop, sidewalk   **Population**: 1

Park near the National Zoo off Connecticut Avenue on one of the side-streets where parking is allowed. Run down through the zoo to the trail which follows the Rock Creek Parkway at the bottom of the hill. Turn left and run north on the park trail which follows the parkway. North of the zoo, the trail turns left, passes through some trees, makes a sharp left turn, and crosses a small causeway over Rock Creek. Run under Park Road, through a meadow, over another small bridge, and directly beside Rock Creek Park Trail. After a few hundred feet, the trail dips into the woods. After coming out from the woods, you will cross a small bridge and pass a playground at the bottom of Tilden Street. Run off the trail near the water fountain and across the meadow toward Tilden Street, which you will see in the distance.

To complete this trail, you will have to run up a steep hill. Turn left on Tilden Street (Park Road) and run to the next traffic light. Turn left on Connecticut Avenue and run down a slight hill to Porter Street through the Cleveland Park shopping area. Cross Macomb Street over a bridge and up a slight grade to the National Zoo whcrc you began.

Special Information: This is a round trip taken over city streets. I included this trail because of its diversity, and especially because of the hill on Tilden Street.

There is a water fountain located near the meadow at the base of Tilden Street. At Tilden Street there is an interesting old gristmill and the Art Barn, where various artists exhibit their work.

Tilden Street — Beach Drive — Military Road
Nebraska Avenue — Connecticut

Location: Northwest Washington, D.C.

Distance: 5.25

Surface: Blacktop, road, sidewalk

Rating: 2

Population: 2

   Start at the corner of Tilden Street and Connecticut Avenue. Run down the steep hill on Tilden Street toward Rock Creek Park. When you reach the bottom of the hill, turn left in front of the Art Barn to reach the Rock Creek Park Trail. The Art Barn is an old carriage house where artists display their work.

   Run north on the trail to Broad Branch Road. Just before reaching Broad Branch Road you will pass picnic areas and parking spots on the right. Run across Broad Branch Road and follow Beach Drive. The paved part of the trail quickly stops. On weekends and holidays, however, the entire segment of this road from Broad Branch Road to Military Road is closed to traffic for use of hikers and joggers. At other times, you must run on a dirt path beside the road. Just before Military Road, you will pass the Park Police substation on the right. At Joyce Road, run to the left across the stream and cross the road. Run north on a paved trail, keeping the stream on your right. After passing under Military Road, turn left and go up a long hill to Oregon Avenue. Here, you will turn left, run a few feet to the corner of Military Road, and turn right (west). You can run on either side of Military Road, but there is a short distance where there is no sidewalk. At Nebraska Avenue, turn left at the light. Run Nebraska Avenue, which is hilly, to Connecticut Avenue. At Connecticut Avenue, turn left and run along the sidewalk to Tilden Street where you began your run.

Military Road — Maryland Line

Location: Washington, D.C., in Rock Creek Park near the Maryland border
Distance: 5   **Rating**: 2
Surface: Blacktop, dirt trail   **Population**: 2

Park on the west side of Beach Drive in the picnic area immediately north of Military Road. A blacktopped trail starts at Military Road, winds through the picnic area, and continues to follow Beach Drive north. The blacktop trail crosses a small bridge and continues on the west side of Beach Drive to Bingham Drive. Cross to the east side of Beach Drive and run on the worn path along the road. Pass a picnic area and run across Sherrill Drive, which enters from the right. Beyond Sherrill Drive, the road is closed on weekends for running and biking. There is a long uphill to the meeting with Wise Road. Come down a short hill, cross West Beach Drive, and continue on Beach Drive to the Maryland border. The northern end of this drive is also closed on weekends. Here the trail is generally flat, but the path is very narrow along the side of the road. At the Maryland line, turn and run back over the same course.

Special Information: Each picnic area along the trail has a water fountain. This segment of the trail is not as popular as the lower Rock Creek Trail. The best part of this trail is the long run up the grade where you are deep in the woods.

Cathedral Avenue — West Trail — Montrose Park

Location: Rock Creek Park, Washington, D.C.
Distance: 2.9   **Rating**: 2
Surface: Blacktop, sidewalk, dirt   **Population**: 2

Park near Cathedral Avenue and Connecticut Avenue just south of the zoo. Run down the hill along Cathedral Avenue to Rock Creek Park. The sidewalk leads three-quarters of the way down the hill to the Rock Creek Trail. Cross 24th Street where it comes down the hill from the north. Run through the start of the course of exercise stations, following the trail down a hill. Just before a small bridge over Rock Creek, leave the exercise trail and run along the creek on the north side. Stay on the trail along the creek and ignore the trails coming in from the right. Run under the Massachusetts Avenue bridge.

The trail leaves the creek and turns uphill. Follow the curves up the hill past the back entrance to Dumbarton Oaks and enter Montrose Park. Leave the trail and run through Montrose Park, exiting on R Street. Return over the same trail.

Special Information: This is a jogging trail, not a fast running trail. It is a quick way from the area of the zoo to upper Georgetown. Running up Cathedral Avenue to Connectucut Avenue will be a good uphill run. I ran this in the summer a few days after a storm. At that time, there was a small flood under the bridge and a swamp just past the bridge.

Melvin Hazen Park Trail

Location: West and east of the 3000 block of Connecticut Avenue, N.W., in Washington, D.C.

Distance: 2   **Rating**: 3

Surface: Dirt   **Population**: 3

Park on Tilden Avenue, N.W., near the west end of the street. At the west corner of Tilden Street near Reno Road, enter the Melvin Hazen Park Trail. The Potomac Appalachian Club has placed markers along this trail. It starts through a swampy area, then crosses over to higher ground. It is a complete cross-country trail with numerous small hills and turns. A side trail comes in from Rodman Street to the south. At the end of the first segment running east, you will run up some steep wooden stairs, emerging behind a building at 3726 Connecticut Avenue. Run Connecticut Avenue and turn toward Porter Street. At Porter Street cross Connecticut Avenue to the east side, then south, and pick up the trail on the north side of 3701 Connecticut Avenue.

The trail then goes down a steep hill through the woods toward Rock Creek Park. There is a small stream along the trail, which has to be continually crossed on this run. The trail exits into a meadow on the south side of Tilden Street at Park Road.

To return, you can run the same trail or turn north and run through the meadow to Tilden Street. Turn left and run the steep Tilden Street hill. Run the hill to the top, pick up the sidewalk, cross Connecticut Avenue, pass Sedgwich Street, and return to the corner of Reno Road and Tilden Street.

Special Information: There is a water fountain at the edge of the meadow and the Rock Creek Park Trail. This trail is rough and through heavy woods. It is possibly more well-suited for hiking than running.

Soapstone Trail

Location: Northwest Washington, D.C., north of the Van Ness Metro stop

Distance: 2.1   **Rating**: 2

Surface: Dirt   **Population**: 3

Start at the corner of Albermarle Street and Connecticut Avenue, N.W. Run east about one-half block to the National Park Service sign announcing the Soapstone Trail. You have two choices at this point: run down a steep hill into the Soapstone Valley Park, or run a few more feet, turn right, and run down what was once Audubon Terrace. I recommend the second choice, i.e., running down the old right-of-way rather than running into the valley. In the valley, you will have to run crisscrossing a stream. Running on the old right-of-way, you will have to cross a barrier to arrive at Audubon Terrace. Continue running west to a deadend, around a barrier, and down the trail. You must run with care because you will have to cross the small stream in the valley three times. At the bottom of the hill, you can run along the edge of the stream.

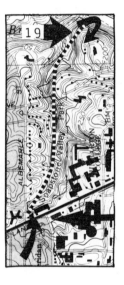

Exit onto Broad Branch Road, turn right, and run a few feet to the Rock Creek Trail. Run the trail south to the Art Barn and Pierce Mill at the corner of Tilden Street and Park Road. Run up this hill on Tilden Street, watching for traffic. When you reach the top of the hill, run right on Connecticut Avenue past the Van Ness Metro stop and shopping center to Albermarle Street and Connecticut Avenue where you began.

Special Information: This is primarily a fast access road to Rock Creek Park from one of the busy areas of Washington.

Beach Drive — Ridge Road

Location: Rock Creek Park, Washington, D.C.

Distance: 3.25

Surface: Road

Rating: 2

Population: 2

    Start on Military Road at the intersection of Oregon and Ridge Roads, N.W. Run south on Ridge Road. The trail leads up the hill toward the Rock Creek Nature Center. Run through the parking lot and continue running south on Ridge Road (Glover Road). Run beside the road past the riding fields. The road curves and drops in elevation to join Broad Branch Road at the bottom of the hill. Turn left on Broad Branch Road. You can return to your starting point the same way or you can run north along Beach Drive to Joyce Street, where you can cross to the north side of the street and run the asphalt trail on the west side of the stream. Pass under Military Road and run west along the north side of the road returning to your starting point at the top of the long hill.

Special Information: Ridge Road (Glover Road) is an outstanding road to run in the winter. After a heavy snow, the road is closed to traffic; when the snow melts, the road remains closed and is great for running. It passes through the center of Rock Creek Park.

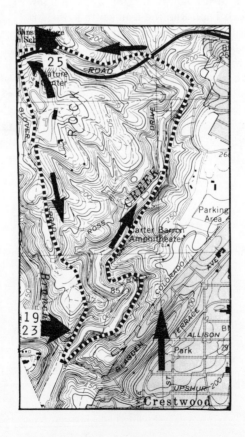

Oregon Avenue — Wise Road

Location: Northwest Washington, D.C., in Rock Creek Park
Distance: 4.5   **Rating**: 2
Surface: Hardtop dirt   **Population**: 2

Park near Military Road and Oregon Avenue, N.W. A blacktopped trail begins on the north side of Military Road and parallels Oregon Avenue along the west side of Rock Creek Park. Run north on this trail. Approximately one-half mile later, the trail crosses a horse path that remains closer to Oregon Avenue, and eventually returns to the blacktopped path just past Bingham Drive. The path for horses is not as smooth—and not recommended. On the blacktopped trail, you will cross a small bridge over the Pinehurst Branch. Just beyond the Pinehurst Branch, run out onto Oregon Avenue and west on Beech Street to Western Avenue. Turn left on Western Avenue and run back into the woods that surround the Pinehurst Branch. The trail is rather poorly marked going back to Oregon Avenue. This section can be jogged but only with difficulty. It is a downhill slope from Western Avenue to Oregon Avenue. Reenter Rock Creek Park where you exited. Continue north to Wise Road, which is as far north as you can easily run.

Beyond Wise Road the trail is more for hiking or easy jogging. The elevation drops quickly once north of Wise Road and the trail is dirt. It becomes difficult to run on. If you continue north, you will exit on Beach Drive near the Maryland border.

The best way to return is to run along the worn path on the north and east sides of Beach Drive until you reach Bingham Drive. At Bingham Drive, the paved path goes along the side and runs west to rejoin the trail along Oregon Avenue. Turn left and run back to your starting point.

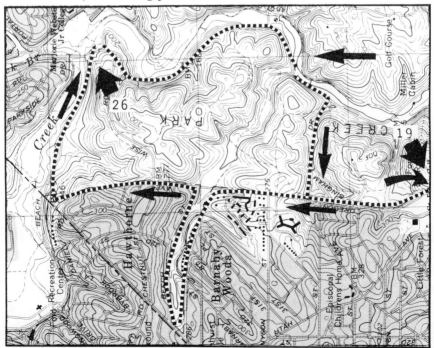

25

West Beach Drive — East Beach Drive — Silver Spring
16th Street — Holly Street Trail

Location: The Northernmost corner of the District of Columbia
Distance: 3   **Rating**: 2
Surface: Road, sidewalk, dirt   **Population**: 2

Start near Parkside Drive and West Beach Drive just below the northernmost corner of Washington. Run north on West Beach Drive, cross a small bridge, and turn left on East Beach Drive. The wooded extension of Rock Creek Park will be on your left. Run north on East Beach Drive until the road turns sharply to the right onto Verbena Street, a residential street. Turn to the right on Verbena Street and run into Tamarach Street. Run left on Tamarach Street for one block to North Portal Drive. Turn left on North Portal Drive and run north one block to 16th Street, N.W., at the Washington, D.C./Maryland line. Turn right on 16th Street and run south approximately 10 blocks to just past Holly Street. Continue one-half block further and Holly Street enters 16th Street from the other side. Opposite the second Holly Street entrance, there is a path to Rock Creek Park. Take this path into the park. It descends to join another trail coming in from the north and continues on to Beach Drive near Riley Spring Bridge. Turn right and run north up the long hill to West Beach Drive and continue to the intersection with East Beach Drive where you began.

Special Information: This run takes you through quiet residential neighborhoods and through the busy 16th Street corridor into Washington, D.C. It also includes a run through the woods of Rock Creek. The entire course is highly runnable.

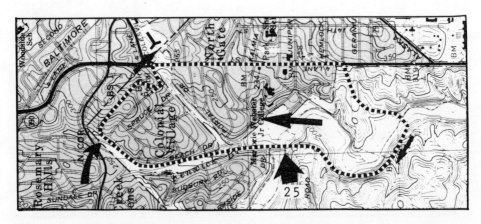

Chevy Chase Circle — Beach Drive
Connecticut Avenue — Western Avenue

Location: Northwest Washington, D.C., and southern Montgomery County
Distance: 9   **Rating**: 2
Surface: Blacktop, sidewalk   **Population**: 2

Park near Chevy Chase Circle at the D.C./Maryland line. Run northwest on Western Avenue, which is the border between the District and Maryland. Run along the sidewalk on Western Avenue to Chestnut Street just a mile beyond Chevy Chase Circle. Turn right and run along Chestnut Street past Oregon Avenue. Chestnut Street eventually becomes Wise Road. Continue running along Wise Road down into Rock Creek Park.

Turn left on Beach Drive and run down a grade, staying on the south side of Rock Creek. Pass to the south of the bridge crossing Rock Creek and stay on the worn path on the north side of the road. Cross the D.C./Maryland line at the large Rock Creek National Park Service sign which faces south.

Continue running along the north side of Beach Drive until you see a bike path sign pointing right across Rock Creek. Follow this path over a running bridge, and through a parking lot. Follow the bike path signs to the right and then left past the Meadowbrook Stables of the Maryland-National Capital Park and Planning Commission to East-West Highway. Cross East-West Highway to the blacktop trail. Pass the Ohr Kodesh Synagogue through an open area and run under a railroad trestle into a wooded area that is swampy in wet weather. You will now be running beside Jones Mill Road. If you do not want to follow the bike path after entering Maryland, you could run Beach Drive-Jones Mill Road to this point. Continue running on the path. When the path breaks down under the beltway, stay to the left. The path picks up on the other side.

Next, you will approach Connecticut Avenue. Turn left and run onto Connecticut Avenue. Be careful at this point, as the sidewalk does not start until the top of the hill at Kensingston Street. Continue north along Connecticut Avenue to Chevy Chase Circle, your point of origin.

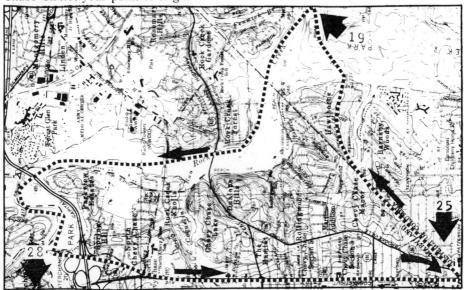

Beach Drive — Connecticut Avenue — Garrett Street

Location: Southern Montgomery County, Maryland, in Rock Creek Park
Distance: 7   **Rating**: 1
Surface: Blacktop   **Population**: 2

Park just east of Connecticut Avenue on the south side of Beach Drive. Run back toward Connecticut Avenue and pass to the south under Connecticut Avenue on Beach Drive. When there have been heavy rains you must pass to the right and cross Connecticut Avenue at the light. You will find the entire area paved, but there is a considerable amount of grass to run on the side. The trail is mostly shade-covered.

Run west from Connecticut Avenue to Cedar Lane, where there is a water fountain. Cross Beach Drive at Franklin Street and enter the woods just to the northeast. Pass through the woods and continue along Beach Drive past two playgrounds. Cross Knowles Avenue and run under the Chessie trestle. Cross Wexford Drive, run through another wooded area, and come back to Beach Drive. Run a small hill to the end of Beach Drive at Garrett Road. Cross Garrett Road to the Viers Mill Recreation Center. There is a water fountain in front of the center and a parking lot.

Special Information: This course is generally flat. There is room to run beside the paved trail and considerable shade. This is an easy trail to follow.

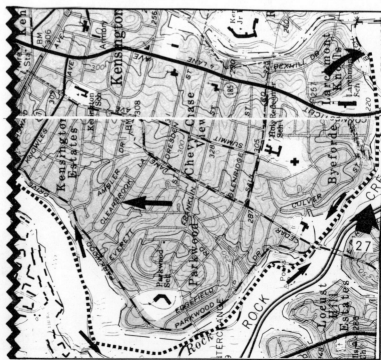

Garrett Road — Norbeck Street

Location: Montgomery County, Maryland, in Rock Creek Park

Distance: 8   **Rating**: 1

Surface: Blacktop   **Population**: 2

Start at Viers Mill Park near Garrett Road. The trail goes through a swampy area and into the woods near Dewey Road. Cross Randolph Road and continue north to a wide meadow with a ball field on the east side. When the trail splits, follow it to the left (west) over a bridge and into the woods. The east trail will take you to Edgebrook Road where Turkey Branch stream runs into Rock Creek. There is no trail connection to Turkey Branch.

Run north on the trail where you will run around a large hill and pass through the woods. Cross over an access road and run parallel to Viers Mill Road. Cross the entrance road to Park Lawn Cemetery and exit eventually at Viers Mill and Aspen Hill Roads. After crossing Viers Mill Road, turn left at Adrian Street (at the first corner) to Battie Avenue and then right on Battie Avenue up a slight hill to the park on the left. Run into the park, keeping to the southwest, where you will see a paved trail. As you continue north along the edge of Rock Creek, you will find another trail on the right (east). This is an access trail leading to Oriental Street, a residential street where parking is available if you only want to run this segment of the trail. Continue running north until you reach Baltimore Road (near Rock Creek High School). This is the only road that you will pass north of Viers Mill Road. Return over the same trail.

Special Information: There is easy running along this trail next to the paved portion on grass. Considerable shade is available. The only water fountain on the trail is at the Recreation Center at Viers Mill Park.

Lake Needwood

Location: Route 28 and Avery Road near Georgia Avenue
Distance: 3
Surface: Dirt, road

Rating: 2
Population: 2

Park near the Visitors' Center at Lake Needwood and begin running counter-clockwise around the lake. Rather than running directly alongside the lake at this point, it is better to run along the access road that parallels the eastern side of the lake. This is due to the absence of a defined trail along the lake once past the Visitors' Center. At the end of this road, you will come to Needwood Road, which runs parallel to the north end of the lake. Turn left on Needwood Road and run just past the west side of the lake. Step over the guardrail and run the grass trail along the west side until you reach another dirt access road coming in from the northwest. Avoid the access roads entering from your right and continue to the south end of the lake. At the south end, cross over the dam and turn north, which will return you to the Visitors' Center.

Special Information: There is water available at the Visitors' Center as well as a telephone. Throughout this run there are a number of trees under which you can rest to avoid the sun. In the summer, there are small boats for lake rides.

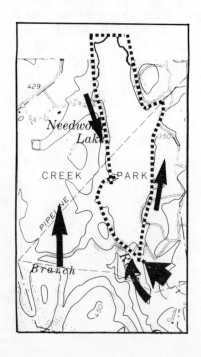

Lake Frank

Location: Seven north of the Beltway off Norbeck and Muncaster Mill Roads in Montgomery County, Maryland
Distance: 8.2   **Rating**: 3
Surface: Dirt, road   **Population**: 3

Park at the Visitors' Center at Lake Needwood. Run south from the Visitors' Center to the southeast corner of the dam. Continue running south through a long grassy area, turn left, and run down into a valley through the woods. Follow a small stream, part of Rock Creek. Soon the trail will turn into a small weeded path which is difficult to maneuver. Next, cross South Lawn Lane and Avery Road and over a small bridge at North Branch. When the trail forks, run to the right and walk up a fairly steep short hill. You will now be at the south end of the dam at Lake Frank. Run to the north on a paved trail away from the dam. After the trail bends away from the lake, run through a parking lot. Continue running along the side of a road staying to the west as much as possible. When you reach another parking lot, cross to the northeast side and find the trail into the woods. From this point north to Muncaster Mill Road, the going will be quite rough: brambles, bugs, and a very uneven trail.

Upon reaching Muncaster Mill Road, run west along the edge of the road to Meadowside Lane, the access road to the Meadowside Nature Center. You can park at the nature center if you want to work out in the Lake Frank area. In midsummer, it is probably a good idea to return by the road as this trail is just too difficult to run easily. Return to Muncaster Mill Road and turn left. Run 0.7 miles to Avery Road and then turn south to Needwood Lake Road approaching from the west. You will run by a large farm estate. Needwood Lake Drive deadends at Beach Drive. Turn left on Beach Drive to return to the Lake Needwood Visitors' Center.

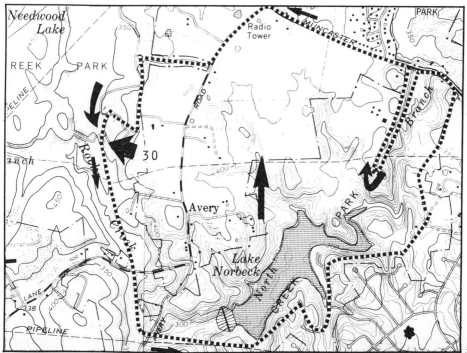

Chapter 4
Mount Vernon Trail

The Mount Vernon Trail is a 17-mile trail starting at the Lincoln Memorial and ending in Virginia at Mount Vernon, the home of George Washington. This trail has a blacktop surface and is excellent for running. There is a break in the trail at Old Town Alexandria, Virginia, where you have to run on city streets. Other than this section in Old Town, the trail has no street crossings.

The trail begins at Memorial Bridge which was constructed in 1932. Just before reaching the 14th Street Bridge, the trail circles behind the Navy-Marine Memorial, a statue dedicated to those Americans who served at sea. South of the 14th Street Bridge, the trail follows the western edge of National Airport and then passes the Washington Sailing Marina, a good place to relax. Next is Old Town Alexandria, an old port city with numerous historic buildings and cobblestone streets dating from colonial times. South of Alexandria the trail crosses over a small portion of Dyke Marsh. The southern terminus of the trail is at Mount Vernon, the home of George Washington. Mount Vernon has been restored to its condition at the time of George Washington's presidency. Even though this trail runs near the George Washington Parkway, it passes through woods, meadows, and marshes. There are numerous hikers, bicyclists, joggers, and runners along the entire length. It is a good trail to observe all of these people. If one wants to go further than 17 miles, the Rock Creek Park Trail joins the Mount Vernon Trail at the Lincoln Memorial, as well as several other trails throughout the course.

There are mileage markers along the trail except for the segment through Old Town Alexandria. It is an excellent trail for running—grass, shade, and water are available along its entire length.

Lincoln Memorial — Iwo Jima Memorial — Pentagon

Location: Arlington County, south of Rosslyn
Distance: 4   **Rating**: 1
Surface: Blacktop   **Population**: 1

Park near the Lincoln Memorial on Ohio Drive or on the Rock Creek Parkway approach to the memorial. After crossing Memorial Bridge on the south side, turn right on the path which crosses the road approaching the traffic circle from the south; run behind the traffic circle.

Cross to the north side of the road. Pass the Metro subway stop and the Seabee statue. Just to the west of an approach ramp from the north there is a blacktopped trail. Run down the trail along the approach ramp and continue north along the boundary of Arlington Cemetery. Follow the path to the northeast edge of the cemetery, turn left, and run west past two small trees growing out of the middle of the trail. Turn right onto the access road for the Iwo Jima Memorial, noting the Carillons to the left. Continue on the approach road to the Iwo Jima Memorial. Circle the memorial and return to the traffic circle by the same trail, except that you will cross the approach road to Arlington Cemetery to the south side instead of running back across the bridge.

On the next leg of your run, proceed to the south approach road. Run on the gravel trail on the east side following the Metro tracks. Eventually you will come to a small tunnel leading to Route 110. Run through the tunnel into the Pentagon north parking lot. Turn left, follow the edge of the parking lot, and run up the dirt path on the small hill to the freeway leading northeast away from the Pentagon toward Memorial Bridge. There is a sidewalk on the south side of the road. Run past the District of Columbia sign on the small bridge and cross the George Washington Parkway approach to Memorial Bridge. You will eventually return to Memorial Bridge.

Special Information: This path should not be run at night as the lights are not sufficient for safe running. Water is available behind the Lincoln Memorial near the refreshment stands and at the information stand at Arlington National Cemetery. This is not a good trail for hot-weather running as it has little shade.

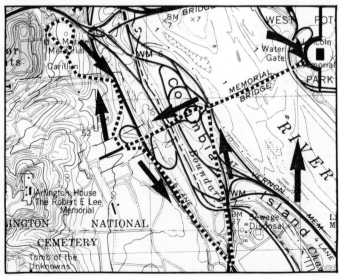

Lincoln Memorial — National Airport

Location: Arlington County south of Memorial Bridge and north of National Airport
Distance: 8   **Rating**: 1
Surface: Blacktop   **Population**: 1

Park near the Lincoln Memorial on Ohio Drive on the Rock Creek Parkway approach to the memorial. Cross Memorial Bridge on the south side. Run along the east side of the traffic circle and continue south. Cross the highway approach to Memorial Bridge and follow the bike path.

Do not take the trail that cuts to the right from this bike path toward the Pentagon. Instead, run toward the trees and the Potomac River. The path goes around behind the Navy-Marine Memorial. Cross over the Boundary Channel lagoon, under the 14th Street Bridge, and past the airport observation parking area close to National Airport. Running or jogging into National Airport is possible from a number of entrances off the trail.

Special Information: The Lyndon Johnson Memorial Grove is south of Memorial Bridge on the opposite side of the George Washington Parkway. The Navy-Marine Memorial is in the same vicinity and is worth a closer look as you run past.

The entire trail is fairly flat. Most of the trail has considerable grassy sections to run on. Also, there is some shade.

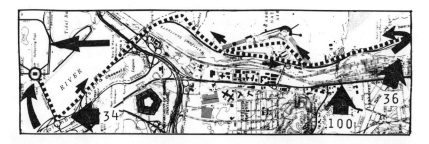

National Airport — Belle Haven

Location: Alexandria, north and south of Old Town Alexandria
Distance: 8   **Rating**: 2
Surface: Blacktop   **Population**: 1

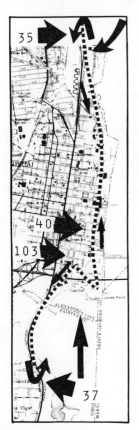

Park at the marina on Daingerfield Street Island one mile south of National Airport. There are recreation fields and a parking lot near the path. Begin running north from the parking lot staying close to the George Washington Parkway. Run across the bridge to the airport past the spot where Four-Mile Run Trail joins the path. Upon reaching the airport, turn back to the south, reaching the point where you parked. Continue south past the recreation fields where, in early summer, ball games will be underway. The trail separates after the section described above. Part of the trail continues north, taking you into Alexandria along Washington Street; the other branch goes off to the east toward Mount Vernon. This part of the trail is relatively new. Take the east branch and run across a plank bridge and behind a large apartment complex. A porch to the power plant located on the Potomac River carries the path over the river behind the plant and around a bend to Fairfax and Third Streets in Alexandria. Follow the railroad tracks south past a city park and onto Union Street. Stay on Union Street and follow the trail east and then south through the woods to the Jones Point access road under the Woodrow Wilson Bridge. Jones Point is a very pleasant park, except that as of June 1984, the road was full of material left over from the reconstruction of the Woodrow Wilson Bridge. At Jones Point is the southern D.C. boundary and the old Jones Point Lighthouse. Continue west to where the trail separates at Royal Street and the access road to Jones Point.

Follow the bike trail under the I-95 approach to the Woodrow Wilson Bridge. Turn west on South Street and then south along the George Washington Parkway and cross Hunting Creek. Follow this path to the Belle Haven Marina. At Belle Haven, reverse your course and return to your point of origin.

Special Information: The trail to the south of Daingerfield Island has considerable shade and interesting terrain, both marsh and manmade. There is a Park Police "trail watch" designed for runners along this path; however, it is not easy to find a phone. There is a water fountain on Daingerfield Island but it is not convenient to the trail.

Belle Haven — Collingwood Boulevard

Location: Fairfax County along the George Washington Parkway toward Mount Vernon
Distance: 6   **Rating**: 1
Surface: Blacktop   **Population**: 2

Park in the Belle Haven parking lot. The trail heads south along the George Washington Parkway and crosses a long bridge over part of the Dyke Marsh before turning back along the parkway. This part of the trail is gently rolling and moves in and out of the woods. There is not much room to run off the trail in this area. You will soon come to a side road which the trail follows (North Down). The trail crosses to the east side of the George Washington Parkway on South Down Road near Alexandria Avenue which enters from the west. The trail heads south along the west side of the parkway through a grassy meadow area. There is not much shade here, but there is considerable grass on which to run.

At Collingwood Boulevard, stop and return to Belle Haven to the north.

Special Information: At Belle Haven there are water fountains on the outside of the restrooms located southeast of the parking lot. There is considerable shade for half of this run. The remainder is primarily in the open. Fill up on water at the drinking fountains next to the restrooms at Belle Haven as there will be no additional water until you reach Fort Hunt to the south.

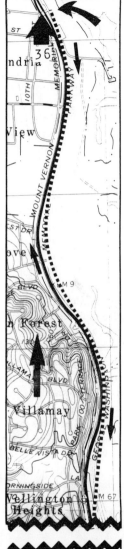

Collingwood Boulevard — Mount Vernon

Location: Fairfax County, south of Alexandria
Distance: 8
Surface: Blacktop

Rating: 1
Population: 2

Park in the vicinity of Collingwood Boulevard and the Mount Vernon Parkway and begin running south. When you reach Waynewood Boulevard the trail becomes hilly. Just past the three-mile marker the trail joins the access road to Fort Hunt Park and Fort Hunt Road. If you wish to run Fort Hunt Park, see the section later in this chapter. Run along the road marked "to Washington." Run through the tunnel and turn right onto the continuation of the Mount Vernon Trail. You will be running on the east side of the George Washington Parkway. Just before milepost 2 there is a water fountain on the west side of the trail. The trail here is rolling and reaches the edge of the Potomac River.

Just before milepost 1 you will run down a slight grade to Riverside Park which has picnic tables and a drinking fountain. The trail circles around the edge of the park and returns to the parkway near Little Hunting Creek. The trail then dips into the woods, runs along a fence up a steep hill, and comes out at milepost 0 at the south end of the Mount Vernon parking lot. There is another water fountain just north of the second parking lot near the road. The George Washington Parkway stops at Mount Vernon. Run around to the front of the estate where you will find restrooms and a water fountain near the gift shop. You can run past the estate, cross the road to the north side, and continue along the east side of Mount Vernon Memorial Highway (north) to Old Mount Vernon Road. This is a blacktopped path with limited room to run on the side. You must return back to your starting point along the same route and the trail is not recommended beyond Mount Vernon.

Special Information: There are no lights located along this section of the Mount Vernon Trail. Water can be found at Fort Hunt Park, Riverside Park, and Mount Vernon. Restrooms are located at Fort Hunt Park and Mount Vernon. This segment of trail offers open meadows, hills, and flat runs along a highway. It also provides nice views of the Potomac River at its widest.

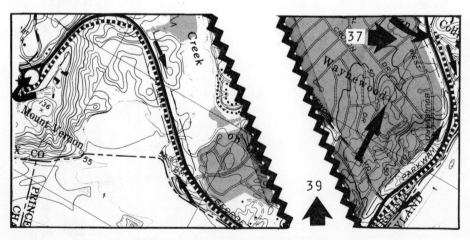

Fort Hunt Park

Location: Northern Virginia, just north of Mount Vernon
Distance: 2.5   **Rating**: 2
Surface: Blacktop   **Population**: 2

Park your car at Fort Hunt Park, which is located directly off the Mount Vernon Trail and the George Washington Parkway, approximately 2.75 miles north of Mount Vernon.

At the park entrance there is a World War I coastal defense gun battery to the left. Locate a cross-road near the ranger's house on the right inside the park. This is the start of the main trail that circles the park. You can run up a path in the middle of the park past the first restroom. Run on the 156 acres of park grass or run on the road circling the park.

Special Information: Fort Hunt is a family picnic grounds with much space for running or jogging. Since the park is flat and provides restrooms and plenty of shade and water, it is a good place for runners who are beginners. There is parking available at the park but it is restricted (by permit) in many areas from Thursday through Sunday. The park closes at dark.

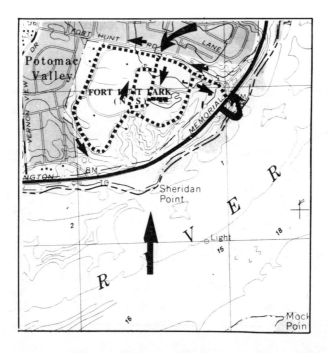

Old Town Alexandria

Location: Northern Virginia, north of the Woodrow Wilson Bridge
Distance: 4   **Rating**: 2
Surface: Sidewalk   **Population**: 1

Old Town Alexandria is an old port city which has been restored. It is now an interesting place to live and visit. There are cobblestone streets, historic homes, fine shops, and restaurants. A run through Old Town is more of a jog than a run because of the number of cross-streets and the number of people on the street.

Park near Washington and Duke Streets, if possible. Run east on Duke Street past the many shops. Just before reaching the Potomac River, run south on Union Street to the end of the street. A trail continues into Jones Point Park, site of an old lighthouse, and the southern cornerstone for the survey of the District of Columbia. Run west under the Woodrow Wilson Bridge to the exit past an old school which is now an Army National Guard Training Command. Run north on Royal Street to Jefferson and then west on Jefferson to Washington Street, the primary route through the city. Run north on Washington Street past Duke Street (where you started) to Oronoco Street. Run east on Oronoco Street to Union Street. Run two blocks south and through the park along the Potomac River. Return to Union Street past the Torpedo Factory, a popular artists' studio and exhibit hall, and back to Duke Street. Run right on Duke Street and then west back to Washington Street where you started. Run back on the opposite side of Duke Street from the side you previously ran down.

Special Information: The reason for running through Old Town Alexandria is to view the town. It is not a particularly great spot for running but, if you are from out of town, it is certainly worthwhile. Another word of caution: Do not run in the evenings or the middle of the weekend because of the number of people on the streets. It is impossible to get through the city at those times. When you run through the city, feel free to detour through historic neighborhoods accessible through side streets. George Washington, Robert E. Lee, and other past leaders of our nation lived in this area.

Chapter 5
The C&O Canal

In 1828, President John Quincy Adams turned the first shovelful of dirt breaking ground for the C&O Canal. As an economic venture, the canal quickly lost ground to the railroads but remained in commercial use until 1924 when a flood seriously damaged the system. Today, the canal runs 185 miles from Cumberland, Maryland, to Rock Creek Park in Washington, D.C. It is maintained by the National Park Service as a multiuse recreational and historical area.

Many people, including the National Park Service, think highly of the C&O Canal trails, and so do I, but they are not exciting for running. In general, the trail is mediocre and can at times be boring for runners looking for a challenge.

In spite of some of its drawbacks, the trail does offer some distinct advantages. First, it is convenient and easy to find even when you are not familiar with the area. Second, it is a good social trail since certain sections are highly populated, especially on weekends. Finally, there are sections of the trail that are very scenic and worth the run just for the beauty of the area.

A final note on the canal itself. If you run the Rock Creek Park to Glover Archbold Park section in winter, it is not uncommon to see green plastic trash bags and assorted garbage standing on the ice-covered canal. This, of course, brings to mind the question of what you miss in the summer when all the trash sinks to the bottom of the canal.

We have divided the C&O Canal area into five running trails. Each segment is unique and will provide a different environment for runners and joggers. The first part, the previously mentioned Rock Creek Park to Glover Archbold Park, is the most populated and social of the group. The next two parts tend to be straight, flat, and dull but do offer fairly secure and accessible trails. The most scenic part is the Carderock to Great Falls trail which can be truly beautiful and is quite secluded. The running section, Great Falls to Pennyfield, is rural and quiet.

Rock Creek Park — Glover Archbold Park

Location: Georgetown in Northwest D.C.
Distance: 2.5   **Rating**: 1
Surface: Brick, dirt, stone   **Population**: 1

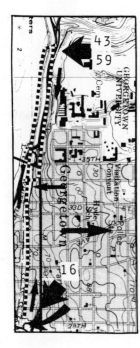

This trail begins behind the Four Seasons Hotel at 2800 Pennsylvania Avenue, N.W., at the junction of Rock Creek and the C&O Canal. The trail begins on the north side of the canal. When running this trail, remember there are a number of cross-streets in Georgetown with heavy traffic.

The brick path at the start of the trail leads past a small park located between Thomas Jefferson Place and 30th Street. In the park there is a bust of Justice William O. Douglas who was responsible for designating the C&O Canal as a national park. Halfway through Georgetown, the trail descends from street level to a level even with the canal. The trail changes from brick to crushed stone and dirt at this point. You will run past an entrance to the Georgetown Park Mall. If the trail is wet or damp, this portion is likely to be muddy.

Before reaching Key Bridge, you will cross over a footbridge to the south side of the C&O Canal. It is easy to run on this part of the trail since it is maintained with red dirt and small stones. Continue to run under Key Bridge which is a primary link between Rosslyn, Virginia, and the District of Columbia.

At a point approximately one-half mile west of the Key Bridge, you will notice a path off to the left. This path leads under the canal and Canal Road and emerges on the Glover Archbold Trail on the north side of Canal Road. If you leave the canal trail, exit on Canal Road. Turn left (east) after emerging onto the road and run back to Georgetown. Canal Road becomes M Street which leads to Pennsylvania Avenue and the Four Seasons Hotel. Because of the congestion on M Street (traffic and pedestrians), you should turn right on 34th Street which will bring you back to the canal.

Special Information: The lower part of the trail is quite old; it dates from 1831. In spite of its age, there are many walkers, joggers, and runners who use it because of its proximity and access to Georgetown. You will still encounter many people even after the trail leaves Georgetown. Runners should be advised of the presence of some rather undesirable characters who sometimes loiter under the bridges along the lower trail in downtown Georgetown. Remember that the trail can also be quite slippery and muddy after a rain. I did not find any drinking fountains along the trail.

Glover Archbold Park — Lock Number 5

Location: Northwest D.C., from Georgetown and just into Maryland
Distance: 7.5
Surface: Dirt, sidewalk

Rating: 1
Population: 2

This part of the C&O Canal Trail starts just southwest of the entrance to Georgetown University on Canal Road. To reach the trail from this spot, go down the cement ramp on the north side of Canal Road and through the tunnel connecting the Glover Archbold Trail with the canal. When you emerge from the tunnel, make a sharp turn to the left and go up a slight rise. The trail will then be in front of you. Turn left and run toward the northwest. From this point until you leave this part of the trail, you will be paralleling Canal Road. When running this part of the trail, commonly known as the Towpath, it is advisable to stay toward the edge of the path.

After two miles, you will pass Fletcher's Boat House and then Chain Bridge. A ramp descends from the walkway along the north side of Chain Bridge. This is part of the Chain Bridge Connector Trail discussed in Chapter 7. The trail crosses into Maryland just north of Chain Bridge. Lock Number 5 of the canal is located approximately one mile north of the bridge. You can leave the path at this point and cut back to a circular cement walk over the George Washington Parkway. This path leads to stairs that end at 61st Street and Ridge Avenue. Run to the left, turn left on Broad Street, right on Maryland Avenue, and up a slight grade to MacArthur Boulevard (see Chapter 7) where you will turn right and head toward Washington, D.C. The actual distance you will run on the C&O Canal Trail will be 3.75 or 7.5, if you double back on the trail. If you leave the trail at Lock Number 5, the trip will be approximately 8 with some small hills to cross running from the C&O Canal and onto MacArthur Boulevard just before reaching the Washington, D.C. line.

Special Information: There are a number of runners from Georgetown University running this trail, but most of them turn around at Fletcher's Boat House. There are also bicyclists on the portions of the trail near Washington. A drinking fountain is available at Lock Number 5. The upper part of the trail cannot be run at night since there are no lights.

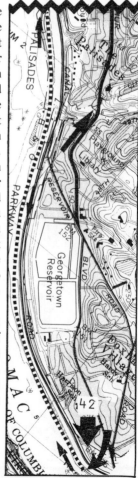

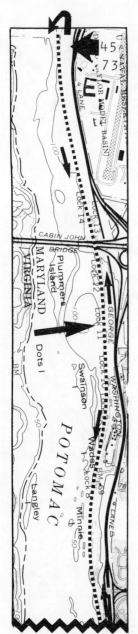

Lock Number 5 — Carderock

Location: Maryland, along the Potomac River from just north of Washington, D.C.

Distance: 10.8   **Rating**: 1
Surface: Dirt, crushed stone   **Population**: 2

Lock Number 5 on the C&O Canal is located in the vicinity of MacArthur Boulevard near Maryland Avenue, just north of the Washington, D.C., line and Dalecarlia Reservoir. To reach this location, drive to the edge of the hill overlooking the George Washington Parkway in Maryland and park as near as possible to 61st Street and Ridge Road. You will find a path there leading down and across a concrete bridge over the George Washington Parkway. Cross the C&O Canal to the trail and turn right.

The portion of the trail from Lock Number 5 to Carderock forms a dike between the Potomac River and the C&O Canal. There are exits from the trail at Glen Echo and Cabin John. Passing under the Beltway, you will see the Navy's David W. Taylor Ship R&D Center. Near milepost 10 on the trail there is a short path leading to the left (west). A parking lot at Carderock is at the end of this path. You can reach this lot by car, exiting the George Washington Parkway in Maryland at the David W. Taylor R&D Center and turning west. There are other accesses to this path at turnoffs from the Maryland George Washington Parkway at the various canal locks.

Special Information: Since this portion of the trail is the least interesting part of the C&O Canal, you will not encounter that many runners or joggers. There are no water fountains north of the one at Lock Number 5.

Carderock — Great Falls, Maryland

Location: Maryland, along the Potomac River, just north of the Beltway

Distance: 6

Surface: Dirt, crushed stone

Rating: 1

Population: 2

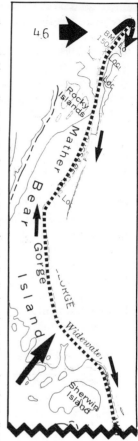

Drive to the parking lot at Carderock by taking the David W. Taylor Ship R&D Center exit off the George Washington Parkway (Maryland). A path leads from the parking lot to the C&O Canal Trail (described in the section covering the trail from Lock Number 5 to Carderock).

At the beginning, run out onto the trail and turn left (north). This is an interesting part of the trail with the Potomac River to the west and the rock formations at Carderock visible along the river. As the Potomac River bends away to the left, the canal widens at a spot called Wide Water. At this point, there is a scenic run along the edge of the canal. Note that the trail soon traverses a large number of rocks in this location and you will have to slow down to a hike for a few hundred yards. This rough area lasts only for a short distance but, because of the problem with rocks on this part of the trail, I have downgraded this segment.

North of the rocky part of the trail, there are many interesting places to stop. You will find a number of signs along the trail which provide details on the various canal locks and the history of the area. As you approach the Great Falls Tavern on the canal, look to your left and observe the force of the water rushing through Great Falls. However, you must be careful of the many sightseers, tourists, and hikers who come to Great Falls and are on the trail for a short distance. Also in the Great Falls region, be careful near those portions of the trail with no guardrail. The National Park Service is in the process of adding additional rails. Cut across the canal at Lock Number 19 and continue up a short path to the Great Falls Tavern and Visitor Center where there are water fountains and restrooms. Behind the Great Falls Tavern is a large parking lot which you can reach by car via MacArthur Boulevard.

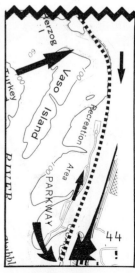

Special Information: Because they are less rocky, the sides of the trail were better for running than the middle. At Great Falls, take some time to walk out over the Potomac at the water intake of the aqueduct dam and view the turbulent force of the river.

Great Falls — Lock Number 22, Pennyfield

Location: Great Falls, Maryland, off MacArthur Boulevard
Distance: 10   **Rating**: 2
Surface: Dirt, crushed stone   **Population**: 3

Start this run at Great Falls Park in Maryland along the Potomac River. Parking is available in a large parking lot located just north of the Great Falls Tavern. Cross the canal to the southwest side and run north. This section of the trail is rather deserted after you run out of the Great Falls area. Note also that there are problems with certain washed-out sections of the trail caused by floods in the spring of 1984.

About a mile and a half north of Great Falls is a large modern water intake plant. When you reach the vicinity of this plant, run to the left along the overlook by the Potomac River. Note the interesting graphic relief tablets illustrating the drop of the Potomac River from the mountains to Chesapeake Bay. When I last ran through this area, I saw one or two people who were lazily drifting and snoozing in canoes in the canal somewhat like a scene from Huck Finn. The canoes were rented from a boat house which you will pass as you run north. From the boat house north, the trail becomes very uneven and rough. There are a number of places where you can twist an ankle if you are not careful. In this segment, I just ran to the 22-mile marker and then back to Great Falls.

Special Information: The boat house mentioned above where canoes are available is at Swains Lock at milepost 16. This section is a good one if you want to get away from people; it is not highly recommended for running or jogging. There are restrooms and a water fountain next to Great Falls Tavern.

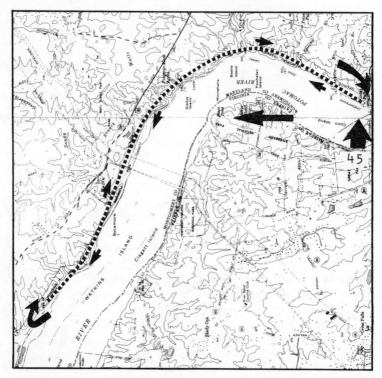

Chapter 6
Washington and Old Dominion Trail

The Washington and Old Dominion (W&OD) Trail stretches from the Potomac River to the Blue Ridge Mountains. The trail traverses the length of the 100-foot-wide W&OD Railroad Regional Park which is part of the Northern Virginia Regional Park Authority. This park was formed from the roadbed of the Washington and Old Dominion Railroad. The right-of-way follows the path of the Virginia Electric and Power Company (VEPCO) power lines which run along the top of the trail from the meeting of Four-Mile Run and I-66 west. Railroad trains ran along what is now the W&OD Trail from 1859 until 1968. The Civil War nearly destroyed the railroad, but it was rebuilt and again became a busy railroad after the turn of the century. The railroad continued to function until 1968, connecting many small towns; these same small towns are now connected by the W&OD Trail. Across the Potomac River from Washington these same towns have now become suburbia, but as you run west, open space is still visible between these "towns." The area located west of Vienna provides the runner with a beautiful view of country life.

The Martha Custis Trail parallels I-66 from Rosslyn to the vicinity of the city of Falls Church boundary. The W&OD Trail is considered by many to follow the Four-Mile Run east to the Potomac River, but with the advent of I-66 and the Martha Custis Trail, I have included the Martha Custis Trail as the first link to the east and treat Four-Mile Run as a separate entity.

I ran this trail from Rosslyn to Sterling, Virginia. The trail has numerous dips along the Martha Custis segment of the trail. The W&OD portion is generally flat. The geographical configuration of this trail is excellent for beginning runners as well as for those who wish to build up their speed. Part of the trail is paralleled by a bridle path. There are bicyclists, hikers, and just strollers on this trail, but there is room enough for everyone.

Rosslyn — Glebe Road

Location: Arlington, at the Virginia end of Key Bridge and running west

Distance: 5   **Rating**: 1

Surface: Blacktop   **Population**: 1

Parking is difficult at the beginning of this trail and the subway is an attractive option for getting into Rosslyn. The Custis Trail starts at the corner of Lee Highway 29-211 and Ft. Myer Drive on the east side of Lee Highway just west of Key Bridge in Rosslyn. At the beginning of the trail you will have to run on a sidewalk. Run west on the north side of the street. At the barrier where Lee Highway crosses Scott Street, you will be on the Custis Trail running beside Lee Highway. When Lee Highway crosses I-66, the trail turns off to the right and follows along I-66. On I-66, the trail cuts from one side of the interstate to the other side and back again. If you run the trail from Rosslyn west, you will run up a curving ramp at Lorcom Lane and I-66. From Lorcom Lane to Glebe Road the trail follows behind the I-66 sound barriers. There are numerous dips in this trail, enough to provide moderate exertion if run at a hard pace.

Special Information: The Custis Trail has a blacktop surface and no shade except at underpasses. It is a new trail; there are many cross-streets with easy access trails spinning off from the trail to the side streets. From Rosslyn to Glebe Road, there is a natural slow rise. There is no water available. The Custis Trail has a minimal amount of grass along the side. When running this trail, you are pretty well confined to the blacktop. This trail can be extremely hot in the middle of the summer because the I-66 pavement is along the side of the trail while blacktop is under foot. This trail is also a bike path. You should watch for bicyclists since they can reach rather high speeds along this route.

Glebe Road — Lee Highway

Location: Arlington, in the vicinity of I-66
Distance: 5   **Rating**: 1
Surface: Blacktop, sidewalk   **Population**: 1

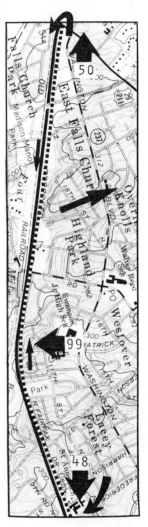

Park on a nearby side street near I-66 and Glebe Road, and locate the trail. From Glebe Road, I-66 heads west paralleled by the Custis Trail. The trail is generally level with some small dips in this segment. At Jacksonville Street, the path dips under I-66 and travels along the south side of the interstate highway. There are two small parks on the south side and an ever-present sound barrier composed of stone on the north side. Near McKinley Road, the Four-Mile Run Trail joins the Custis Trail (see Chapter 9). At Roosevelt Street, the trail leaves I-66 and runs through a park where the trail becomes crushed gravel. The trail turns right and follows the sidewalk along Van Buren Street and 19th Street before rejoining I-66. By taking this detour on the trail, you will avoid the East Falls Church Metro Stop at Sycamore Street. This part of the trail ends at the Arlington-Falls Church boundary at Lee Highway and Fairfax Drive.

Special Information: There is no water along the trail. This can be a very hot trail in the summer, and there is not much shade. This trail is lighted only along I-66. Since there are very few difficult dips, this section is quite satisfactory for the beginning runner or jogger. When running this trail from west to east, do not attempt to take the Sycamore Street detour as it hugs I-66 rather than going through the park. The Metro stop is fenced off and it is difficult to get back on the trail if you take the shortcut. This trail is a high-speed bike trail, so be careful.

Location: Falls Church and Fairfax County
Distance: 8   **Rating**: 1
Surface: Blacktop   **Population**: 2

Park near the intersection of I-66 and Lee Highway and locate the trail. This section of the W&OD Trail starts at Lee Highway and Fairfax Drive and proceeds west to Cedar Lane in Fairfax County. It is a level course with only one slight grade. The trail moves west across Little Falls and Great Falls Roads. From Great Falls Road to West Street in Falls Church, there are four exercise stations. The trail follows Shreve Road to Virginia Lane where it rises up a slight grade to meet and cross I-66. After a few hundred yards, the trail heads northwest and crosses I-495 just north of the point where I-66 crosses the Beltway. The trail crosses Gallows Road before reaching Cedar Lane.

Special Information: The entire trail is blacktop. There are no water fountains available. There are some parking spaces next to the trail on Cedar Lane. Unlike the Martha Custis section of the trail, there is grass along the W&OD Trail so you can run off the trail on the side if you do not want to run on the blacktop.

Cedar Lane — Clarks Crossing

Location: The town of Vienna in Fairfax County, Virginia
Distance: 7   **Rating**: 1
Surface: Blacktop   **Population**: 2

There is a parking space next to this trail at Cedar Lane. As you leave Cedar Lane, run west on the trail. It bends slightly to the right and passes a plant where I noticed numerous employees coming out to run at noontime. After entering the city of Vienna, the trail crosses Park Street. Behind the community center located at Park Street, there is a small cluster of exercise stations. These stations are not as well spaced as some of the stations on other trails. One block past Park Street is Maple Avenue which is the main thoroughfare in Vienna. Maple Avenue is difficult to cross because of heavy traffic in both directions. Follow the signs along the side of the trail directing you to go one block north to cross at Maple Avenue and then run south one block to rejoin the trail. Run west across Church Street. Beside the trail in Vienna is the Freeman House which was used as a hospital during the Civil War. As you leave Vienna, the trail will stretch out in front of you for about one mile. The trail crosses Piney Branch which flows under an ancient stone arch dating from before the Civil War. At the 13-mile marker, Clarks Crossing Road will join the trail on the right.

Special Information: Along Maple Avenue there are establishments where you can pick up a soft drink. There is no water available along this part of the trail. There are bicyclists on this section. It is possible to run on the grassy side on portions of the path. You should not start out on this trail late in the day since there are no lights on a large part of it. There is not much shade available.

Location: Fairfax County, Virginia, west of Falls Church and southeast of Reston

Distance: 6

Rating: 1

Surface: Blacktop

Population: 2

As you run west from Clarks Crossing on this trail, you will have to cross two wooden footbridges. There is a rise to run up to Hunter Mill Road. At Hunter Mill Road there is one parking space next to the trail. West of Hunter Mill Road the trail is relatively rolling until you reach Sunrise Valley Drive. After passing Sunrise Valley Drive and around a bend, you will see the Dulles Access Road. When I ran under the access road in May 1984, I found considerable construction activity underway on the road, but it did not in any way hinder movement on the trail under the road. I stopped at Sunset Hills Road. Look for the George F. Warner Airconditioning Company directly across the road off the trail. There is a sign on the trail just on the other side of Sunset Hills Road pointing out the Warner Building as a place for complimentary water. The drinking fountain is on the outside of the building, and the water is cold.

Special Information: There is not much shade on this part of the trail. The Warner Building is the only site for water available on this part of the trail. There are no lights, making it impossible to run at night. As with other sections of this trail, there are bicyclists you should watch for.

Sunset Hills Road — Herndon

Location: Fairfax County, Virginia, between Reston and Herndon

Distance: 7   **Rating**: 1

Surface: Blacktop   **Population**: 1

When I ran this segment of the W&OD Trail, I parked at the northwest corner at the intersection of Wiehle Avenue in Reston and Sunset Hills Road. A commuter lot is located there with plenty of parking spaces. From this point I ran east to Sunset Hills Road, turned, and ran back to the west. Between Sunset Hills Road and Wiehle Road there is a slight bank to the left; the path follows between two rises on each side of the trail out to what was clearly the old railroad right-of-way. Continue to run south of Reston along this right-of-way. The Reston Country Club golf course will be on your right. As you prepare to leave the Reston area, you will pass the Bowman distillery, home of Virginia Gentlemen, on your left with a number of their buildings on the right. The smell from the distillery will be quite evident in this area. Cross Reston Avenue, run down a dip in the road, and follow a gentle curve to the right. You will soon be out in the country on your way to Herndon. As you leave the south side of Reston, you will notice a bridle path which runs along the side of the trail and crosses over from time to time. There are some houses along the trail on the right as you approach Herndon. Cross Coral and Van Buren Streets in Herndon, then turn and run back when you reach Eldon Street.

Special Information: There is very little shade on this part of the trail. You can fill up with the water available at the Warner Company at Sunset Hills Drive at the start of your run. There are no lights along the trail so you cannot run here at night. Once again, I would like to repeat: This is a bike path, so watch out for high-speed bicyclists. However, when I ran this part of the trail, for the most part, I met only children running at a slow pace.

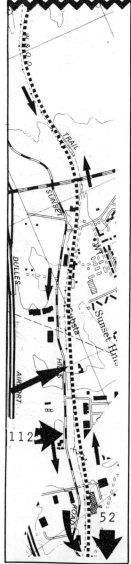

Location: Fairfax and Loudoun Counties, Virginia
Distance: 6.5   **Rating**: 1
Surface: Blacktop, cinder   **Population**: 3

Park in downtown Herndon near Eldon Street and the old railroad station. Run west on the trail past the railroad station toward the industrial side of town. Pass south of a working cement plant about three-quarters of a mile from your starting point to reach a large golf course. You will run by exercise stations in the vicinity of the golf course.

After passing the exercise course, you will reach Crestview Drive. Across Crestview Drive, the trail surface turns to cinders in the vicinity of the Loudoun County line. It is the first change in running surface from the beginning of the trail in Rosslyn. After two miles you will be south of Sterling Park. Continue running south of the park until you reach Church Road, Route 625. Continue across Church Road and stop at Old Church Road just beyond the main road. I found a soft drink vending machine on the porch of a lawn mower company just south of the trail on Old Church Road in Sterling. Return to Herndon over the same trail.

Special Information: There is not very much shade on the trail. I met walkers and bicyclists. This segment is primarily rural and should not be run at night.

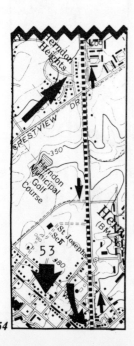

Chapter 7
The District of Columbia

Washington, D.C. is a city whose sights are known to millions. Only a few know it as a city with many enjoyable running trails. Most runners and joggers in the greater Washington area run the sidewalks of the neighborhoods or take to one of the few well-known running trails. Washington has excellent paths and trails to run in each part of the city. Fortunately, there is much more to Washington, D.C. than just these few options. There are deep woods, meadows, and tree-lined streams. There are level trails, excellent for speed work, rolling paths to test your endurance, and fine cross-country trails.

I have separated three of the most popular and most well-known running areas into chapters by themselves, Downtown Sightseeing Runs (Chapter 2), Creek Trails (Chapter 3), and C&O Canal Trails (Chapter 5). This chapter concentrates on the smaller or less well-known trails.

Some of these trails have histories connected with the defense of Washington during the Civil War; others cross the National Arboretum and garden spots of the city. There are paths which follow the park system and trails close to some of the major hotels located in northwest and away from the downtown area.

Most of all, Washington is fun to run because of its interesting geographic and historic diversity. There are numerous cultures represented throughout the various neighborhoods of Washington. So enjoy the total spectrum of running here. This chapter should make it easier for you, but remember, Washington is a big city with big city problems. Use common sense in selecting trails and times to run. Also keep in mind that parking in D.C. is at best a questionable proposition. The Department of Transportation issues tickets seemingly depending more on the color of your car than on your actual infraction. To avoid tickets, check for signs one block in each direction from your car, and hope.

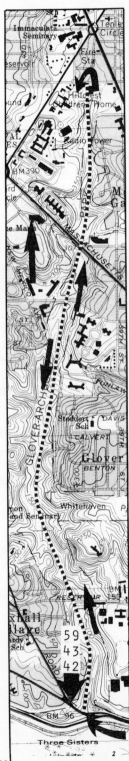

Glover-Archbold Park

Location: Northwest D.C., Georgetown to the National Cathedral

Distance: 7.2   **Rating**: 2

Surface: Packed dirt   **Population**: 3

Start on the north side of Canal Road west of Key Bridge and the entrance to Georgetown University. The entrance to the trail is on the north side of the road behind a small grass-covered park and under a railroad trestle. This segment of the trail consists of a narrow path with vegetation on both sides. At the end of this segment, exit into the grassy park. Look to the left on the hill ahead and you will see a worn path going up the hill. Cross Reservoir Road and pick up the trail to the left across the street. Start down the trail, run down some erosion control steps and across a bridge, and then turn to the left (north). Pass Whitehaven Park Trail along the large clay drainage pipe. The trail becomes wide and straight through the woods. Stay to the right in this segment when you see a trail coming in from the northwest. The trail curves around and exits onto New Mexico Avenue near Garfield Road. Reenter the trail to the left, northwest across New Mexico Avenue, and go down the erosion control steps. The trail winds around, coming out at Cathedral Avenue, and exiting up a short wooden stairway. Cross the street, go through a swampy area, cross Massachusetts Avenue, and run to the right. A large open field is to the northeast. Run along the edge of the woods, keeping the woods to your left (northeast).

Continue to the north; the entrance of the trail is at the northwest corner. Run through a level area and enter the woods. In this segment, you will cross a stream and run up a grade with erosion control steps. The trail then opens out into a meadow where you will find a path across the meadow to take you to Van Ness Street. Return to your starting point over the same course.

Special Information: This is a first-class cross-country running course, one of the best in the city. It has many different variations: hills, stairs, meadow, city sidewalks, etc. The blue blazemarks on the trees marking this trail were placed there by the Appalachian Trail Club.

Watch for traffic when crossing the city streets; these streets are heavily travelled.

Battery Kemble Park

Location: Northwest Washington near American University

Distance: 3   **Rating:** 2

Surface: Worn dirt, fine stone   **Population**: 2

This trail starts at the southwest corner of Foxhall and Loughboro Roads. If you drive, there are numerous places to park on side streets.

There is a grassy park at the corner of Foxhall and Loughboro Roads where you will begin your run. Proceed into the park to a dirt trail which descends steeply through some woods and opens onto a grassy field. Run to the left of a dirt road that enters the field from the other side. Continue descending on the path toward MacArthur Boulevard. This is a short but pleasant cross-country type trail with a small stream visible to the left and some rather large houses in view through the woods. This is a good hot weather course because of the dirt surface and the abundance of shade provided by the woods. The trail ends at MacArthur Boulevard.

To pick up the next trail, run to the right (north) along MacArthur Boulevard and the edge of the park to Chain Bridge Road. At Chain Bridge Road, pick up on a trail to the right (away from MacArthur Boulevard and to the north). You can run this trail north intersecting the dirt road leading into the grassy park. Continue across the road to rejoin the Battery Kemble Park trail and return to the starting place. If you find the hill a little steep, just walk back; there is no stigma to walking when the going gets rough.

At MacArthur Boulevard, you may notice a dirt trail on the other side of the street. This trail starts across the street from the finish of the Battery Kemble Park trail. The trail leads to the edge of a cliff, turns north, and comes out on Nebraska Avenue. You can then run Nebraska Avenue back to MacArthur Boulevard and end directly across from Chain Bridge Road. A word of caution: Walking is recommended. The steep drop along the cliff and the possibility of slipping or tripping make it dangerous to run or jog.

Special Information: There are no lights on this trail; it cannot be run after dark. Remember that, while there is considerable shade, there is no water, and that the trail is packed dirt and fairly rough.

Chain Bridge Connection Trail

Location: Northwest Washington, south of the Maryland line
Distance: 2.2   **Rating**: 3
Surface: Dirt, sidewalk   **Population**: 2

If you are running in Virginia near the Potomac River or in the northwest section of the District of Columbia, it is possible to cross to the other side and pick up other trails described in the District of Columbia and Virginia chapters.

Chain Bridge connects the two banks of the Potomac River. In Virginia, it is located at the end of Glebe and Chain Bridge Roads. Cross Chain Bridge Road on the sidewalk on the north side of the bridge. Take the steps near the end of the bridge leading down from the bridge to connect with the C&O Canal Trail. Cross the George Washington Parkway carefully at this point since there is no crosswalk. You will see a dirt path going up the side of the hill in front of you. The start of the trail is just to the left of the walkway across Chain Bridge. You will have to run up a steep hill on a path which doubles back to reach the top. You will cross a railroad track and, when you reach the top, you will have to step over a low cable barrier. You will come out on Potomac Avenue at the base of Manning Place. Run Manning Place north, cross MacArthur Boulevard, and continue up a grade on Manning Place until you reach Palisade. Turn left on Palisade and run to Loughboro Road. Loughboro Road connects with Massachusetts Avenue and Nebraska Avenue at Ward Circle. This is the neighborhood where you find the campus of American University. From this point, it is easy to connect with numerous trails in northwest Washington.

Special Information: The trail up the side of the hill is not good for running, but it is a way of reaching northwest Washington without having to run on busy roads. There are no lights on the trail up the hill, so do not try to run this trail at night. Also, you should not cross the George Washington Parkway (Maryland) in the dark.

MacArthur Boulevard, D.C.

Location: Northwest D.C., from the Maryland border to Georgetown
Distance: 6.2   **Rating**: 2
Surface: Primarily sidewalk   **Population**: 2

MacArthur Boulevard within the District of Columbia is a link between the MacArthur Boulevard Trail in Maryland and downtown areas. MacArthur Boulevard may also be used to return to the city after running on the C&O Canal Trail. It is worth running even though the path is primarily on sidewalk. If you are only going to run one direction on this trail, it is easier to run from north to south because of a slight drop to the south. There are no large hills on this route; however, there is a small hill where the trail ends by Canal Road.

Starting in the north, the route begins at the Maryland border in front of the Dalecarlia Reservoir on the west side of MacArthur Boulevard. After passing the light at Loughboro Road and Arizona Avenue, cross to the northeast side of the street. The sidewalk is missing for a short stretch in that location. Continue running on the north side of the street and, upon reaching the Georgetown Reservoir, keep to the right staying on MacArthur Boulevard; Reservoir Road and MacArthur Boulevard merge for a very short way, and it is possible to make a mistake. Run down a short hill and join Canal Road on the right. The Glover-Archbold Park Trail merges on the left shortly after MacArthur Boulevard joins Canal Road. You will find the Glover-Archbold Park Trail in a small grassy area on the left. If you run straight ahead on Canal Road, you will enter Georgetown.

To return to your point of origin, it is best to run MacArthur Boulevard in reverse. It is a different trail when running north because of the slight uphill grade.

Special Information: This trail can be run in the evening as the neighborhoods you pass are more like small towns than the big city of Washington. There is no water available, but there are some soft drink vending machines. Although this is a sidewalk trail, it joins numerous other paths, making it of considerable value and interest to runners.

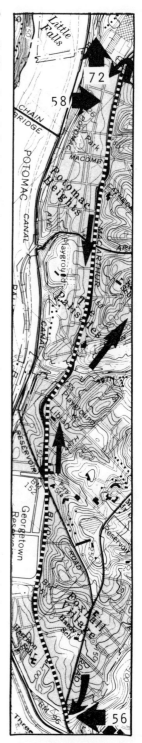

Fort Mahan — Fort Dupont Park

Location: Southeast Washington near East Capitol Street and Branch Avenue
Distance: 5.5   **Rating**: 2
Surface: Crushed gravel   **Population**: 2

This trail makes up one-third of the National Park Service's Fort Circle Park. The other two sections are Fort Dupont to Branch Avenue and Branch Avenue to Suitland Parkway. I run this entire system as one trail. However, because of the number of hills and the difficulty and length of the entire course, I have divided it into three sections.

Park on 42nd Street, N.E., near Gault Street. You can also reach the start of this trail by subway on the Orange Line to Minnesota, or the Blue Line to Benning Road. There is a path to the north of Gault Street, but because of the number of cross-streets and pedestrians, this is not a good path for running. Run south on 42nd Street along a blacktopped path to a crushed gravel path on your right. This path circles Fort Mahan Park. After circling the park on this path, run down the small hill on the north side of the park through the grass and across Benning Road. Continue south along the edge of 41st Street into a small park and past a playground. Cross East Capitol Street carefully and enter Fort Chaplin Park. The trail winds through Fort Chaplin Park and exits just to the east of Weatherless Elementary School at Burns and C Streets S.E. Cut west across C Street and into the park.

The trail exits near the south corner of Texas and Ridge Roads. Cross Ridge Road and enter Fort Dupont Park which is the highlight of this particular trail. It consists of deep woods with a considerable number of hills. The end of Fort Dupont Park is at Massachusetts Avenue, N.E.

Special Information: The Fort Circle Trail connects a ring of forts built during the Civil War to protect Washington from the Confederate forces. The Fort Dupont section of the trail is impressive, but the level of upkeep on the path is disappointing. This could present problems to the runner as could the trash strewn along 40th Place and on the trail itself. *Important*: All three of the Fort Circle Trails are in relatively high crime areas and should never be run alone or at night.

Fort Dupont — Ridge Road — Branch Avenue

Location: Southeast Washington at Fort Dupont
Distance: 3.75   **Rating**: 2
Surface: Crushed gravel   **Population**: 3

I included Fort Dupont in the description of the course that I recommended for the run from Fort Mahan to Fort Dupont. Fort Dupont is a great trail and can be the connector for the two sections.

Park near Ridge Road in southeast Washington. Because the woods are deep and the trees are large, this is a good hot weather trail. Cross Massachusetts Avenue and find the trail at the edge of the woods. It is paved for a short distance. You can run on the grass next to the trail if you prefer into Fort Davis Park. The paved trail follows along the side of Fort Dupont Drive. As it moves away from the road, it becomes a crushed stone trail again. Cross Pennsylvania Avenue and exit eventually on Branch Avenue. Return to the point of origin over the same trail.

Special Information: There are no lights on this trail. It should not be attempted after dark. This section is the most runnable of the entire length of the Circle Trail and there are very few people on the trail. However, there are several muddy spots in the woods after a rain and the section of the trail to the north has some rough spots and a number of cross-streets. You will find that the section of the trail to the south is a real cross-country trail. There is considerable shade but no water on any part of the Circle Trail. **Important**: All three of the Circle Trails are located in relatively high crime areas and should never be run alone or at night.

Branch Avenue — Suitland Parkway

Location: Southeast Washington in the Good Hope neighborhood
Distance: 3   **Rating**: 3
Surface: Crushed gravel, dirt   **Population**: 3

Park near the intersection of Branch Avenue S.E. and the Circle Trail to get to the area of the trail. Run along the west side of Branch Avenue and turn right (west) onto Park Drive. The Circle Trail continues off Park Drive into the woods. Cross 28th Street and run through the park exiting near Naylor Avenue and 27th Street. Cross Naylor Avenue and go back into the woods. Exit the woods and cross on Good Hope Road. The Fort Circle Trail will take you into Fort Stanton Park.

The entire Circle Trail is hilly, but this particular section is more rolling than any other part. The trail exits on Fort Place near Bruce Place Southeast. When exiting the trail, you must run down a grassy hill to Fort Place. (The R&D Center for the Anacostia Smithsonian Center is across the street on Fort Place.) Run across the street and to the right (west). Run through the picnic tables on the west side of the R&D Center and into the woods. This area is not part of the National Park Service and, at first glance, it is rather difficult to find the trail. If you run south in the woods along 18th Place, you will find an old overgrown street which you can follow through the woods and up a slight hill. Notice that from the top of this small hill you can hear traffic on the Suitland Parkway in the distance. Work your way southeast and exit the woods on 22nd Street. Run down 22nd Street to Irving Street and follow a short dirt trail to Suitland Parkway.

The entire Circle Trail is good to run except for the last section, which is not under the auspices of the National Park Service. There is considerable trash dumped on 22nd Street. Reaching Suitland Parkway is also a challenge because of the overgrown adjacent section. To return to your starting point, follow the trail in reverse order.

Special Information: Since there are no lights on the trail, it cannot be run after dark. Also, there are no drinking fountains or comfort stations. **Important**: All three of the Fort Circle Trails are located in relatively high crime areas and should not be run alone or at night.

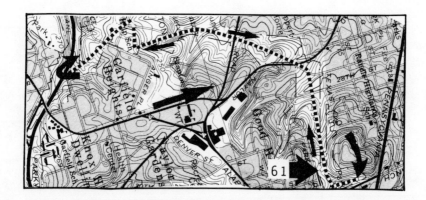

Anacostia Riverfront

Location: Southwest D.C., north of the Douglass Bridge. When driving, cross the Anacostia River on the Douglass Bridge (South Capitol Street). Turn right immediately after crossing the bridge. Stay to the right when you reach the river. This last turn places you on the road through the park.

Distance: 5.5   **Rating**: 2

Surface: Dirt path, paved road   **Population**: 1

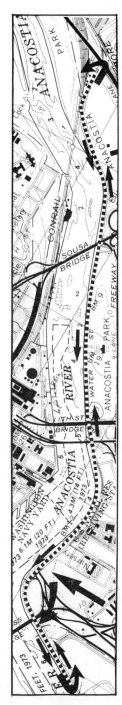

Park just north of the Anacostia Naval Station and the Frederick Douglass Bridge. Run south from where you park to the fence that marks the northern edge of the Naval Station. Just north of the fence run on grass along a dike constructed by the Corps of Engineers for control of the Anacostia River. Continue running north along the west side of the Anacostia Park on a path through the grass.

Just south of the old Civilian Conservation Corps Buildings and the Navy Annex located by Good Hope Road, cut to the other side of the road and run on the sidewalk. Pass under the 11th Street Bridge. When the sidewalk ends, cut back across the road and run the worn path through the grass past the parking spaces and picnic tables. The Anacostia Park Recreation Center is on the east side of the road. Continue running north and pass under the Pennsylvania Avenue Bridge. A large recreation center will be on the right in the middle of the park. There is a water fountain on the north side of this building. Continue north on the trail to the dirt road marked for government vehicles only. This road follows the railroad tracks. Because these tracks are used by a busy railroad system, you should follow the crushed stone road rather than the dirt trail which cuts across the tracks. This route will bring you to the end of the trail. Follow the same path back to your starting point.

Special Information: Problems may arise in the future in the area of the Anacostia Park Recreation Center when the Metro's Green Line system begins subway construction through the park. This park is part of the National Park Service System and closes at dark. This trail is in a relatively high crime area and should not be run alone or at night.

Kenilworth Park

Location: Northeast D.C. in the Mayfair-Parkside neighborhood, west of the Anacostia Freeway and south of the Aquatic Gardens
Distance: 3   **Rating**: 2
Surface: Paved walk, road, dirt   **Population**: 3

The entrance to Kenilworth Park is located off Kenilworth Avenue and Bouroughs Street. On many maps Bouroughs Street is still shown as Deane Street. Drive through the entrance road and park at any number of places where you can pull off the road.

Run back to the park entrance. There is a blacktopped trail that parallels the entrance road on the left side of the drive. This initial opening into the park has a number of trees providing sufficient shade. Run past an old metal gate located approximately 100 yards into the park to a wagon trail on the left. Along the trail is a par course exercise area donated by the J.C. Penney Company. When I last ran this course, the general area was mowed, but the par course stations were fairly overgrown and in disrepair. Stay on the trail past the access road, cross the road, and follow the path along the Anacostia River. Run up a slight rise, cross the road once again, and pass the comfort station where there is a water fountain. Follow a small stream and return to the main road which you previously crossed.

Special Information: Kenilworth Park is maintained by the National Park Service. There are shelters, restrooms, and water fountains available. The park closes at dark. Other than the shelters for picnics, there is not much shade in the park. Frankly speaking, I think additional efforts are needed for maintenance in the park. For instance, grass is sometimes not mowed down enough to make running easy. The roadbed of the trail is generally rough but presents no real difficulty for running. This trail is located in a relatively high crime area and should not be run alone or at night.

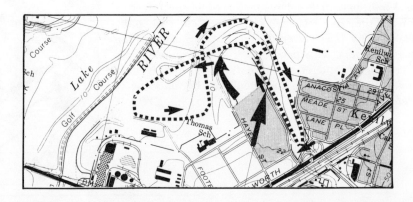

Kenilworth Aquatic Gardens

Location: Southeast part of D.C. It is on the east side of the Anacostia River. Take Douglass Street from Kenilworth Avenue and follow the signs.

Distance: 2   **Rating**: 2
Surface: Packed dirt   **Population**: 2

Park at the entrance to the Aquatic Gardens in the National Park Service's parking lot on Anacostia Avenue opposite Ponds Street. A dirt path leads from the parking lot to the gardens. I ran this area at approximately 10 a.m. on a Sunday morning and found it fairly congested. The best time to view the gardens in bloom is before the heat of the day. The gardens cover 90 acres with 40 pools of aquatic plants.

When you enter the gardens, cut to the left and run down the left side, making a circle on the outside of the ponds. After circling the gardens, run back into the center and through the area containing the various ponds. There is another less-developed path that starts on the northeast side of the gardens and heads out into the marsh and islands. I met two other runners on this trail. The trail deadends in about half a mile at the edge of the Anacostia River. This is an isolated marsh area, home to various species of wildlife. Return to the gardens over the same trail.

Special Information: The Aquatic Gardens became part of the National Park Service system in 1938. There are two different times of the year when the park should be visited. In June, approximately 70 types of day-blooming water lilies are in bloom. Toward the end of July and into August, about 30 varieties of day-blooming and 12 varieties of night-blooming tropical water lilies are in bloom. Park Rangers conduct tours and explain the various plants to different groups. This area is not recommended for running after dark or alone. Also, since you are running along one of the marshy areas of the Anacostia River, there may be a problem with ticks at various times of the year.

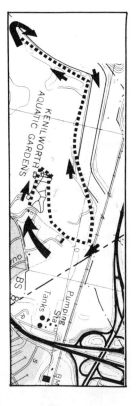

National Arboretum

Location: Northeast D.C., west of the Anacostia River. The main entrance is off New York Avenue, on the south side east of Bladensburg Road.

Distance: 4.3   **Rating**: 1
Surface: Blacktop roadway   **Population**: 2

Enter the main gate of the Arboretum from New York Avenue and drive halfway around the arboretum to the southeast corner and find a place to park.

Proceed to run the circumference of the park. You can begin by running the Rhododendron Valley road to a parking lot, north through the parking lot, and, in the summer, past the National Garden which demonstrates how to grow small outdoor gardens and abundant plants in apartments. Turn right past this garden to Crabtree Road. Turn right and follow a dirt road that looks as if it is an access road for the construction work around the garden. This trail leads down to the Anacostia River. Run up a hill to return to a "normal" path on Hickey Hill Road. Stay to the right, run past the dwarf conifers, and then to the left down Conifer Road. Run Springhouse Road to Hickey Lane, pass the administrative entrance, and back to Azalea Road where you began.

A runner through the arboretum should stay as close as possible to the outside. If you want to clock a large number of miles, there are numerous cross-streets. The speed limit is 15 miles per hour, so running on the road is very safe. It is possible also to run on the grass along the side of the road.

Special Information: The National Arboretum is open from 8 a.m. to 5 p.m., Monday through Friday; and 10 a.m. to 5 p.m., Saturday and Sunday. There are some excellent exhibits to view inside the building when you have finished running. The arboretum is good for running; most of the roads are gently rolling. There are numerous drinking fountains throughout the area. The National Arboretum is operated by the Department of Agriculture, not the Park Service.

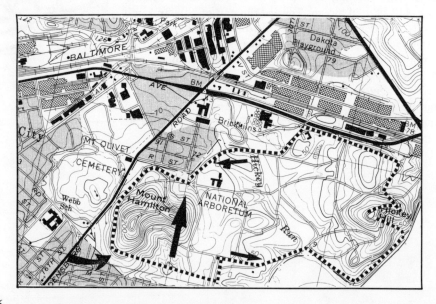

Fort Totten — Fort Slocum — Fort Stevens

Location: Northwest D.C., east of Rock Creek Park
Distance: 5.25   **Rating**: 2
Surface: Grass, sidewalk   **Population**: 2

Park your car on Colorado Avenue, N.W., just southwest of 13th Street. Begin running toward 13th Street and turn north until you come to Fort Stevens at the corner of Quintana Street and Piney Branch Road. Run north on 13th Street beside the fort and turn right on Quintana Street.

Run right on Quintana Street and cross in front of a school. Continue running across Georgia Avenue and then run on the grass after crossing to the south side of Quackenbos Street. The best strategy for running this course is to stay on the grass. Cross 9th Street moving once more to the south and run across Peabody and 8th Streets to the east side of 8th Street. Turn left as you approach Missouri Avenue. Running north on Missouri Avenue, cross 5th Street and stay south of Madison Street. Run north as you cross 3rd Street, N.W.

Run north across Kansas Avenue and North Capitol Street and turn south. After one block, turn left on MacDonald Place. Run through the small park behind the houses along the left side (east) of the street and then back to the street. Turn left (east) when you reach Riggs Road and then run right immediately toward the Fort Totten Red Line subway stop. As you approach the station, look for an asphalt path to the southwest away from the station. Follow the path around to the left uphill into Fort Totten Park. Take the path that loops through the middle of the woods past some ancient breastworks. Eventually you will exit the woods on an access road which comes out of the park on Fort Totten Drive. Proceed south along the east side of Fort Totten Drive running downhill. Stop at Urell Street.

To return to your starting point run Fort Totten Drive north to the intersection of Missouri Avenue and Riggs Road. Turn left on Missouri Avenue and return to Georgia Avenue. Go north one-half block to Military Road and then one-half block west to return to Colorado Avenue.

Special Information: There are lights along this trail on the street but not in the woods, so running here after dark is not recommended. There is no actual path for much of this trail, but there is considerable grass to run on.

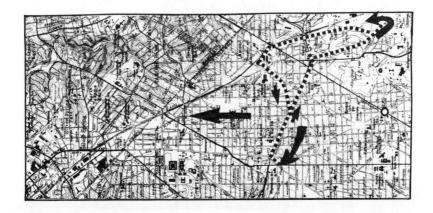

Garfield Road — Connecticut Avenue

Location: Northwest Washington, north of Rock Creek Park
Distance: 5   **Rating**: 1
Surface: Sidewalk, packed dirt   **Population**: 1

Start from the corner of Connecticut Avenue and Woodley Road by the Sheraton Washington Hotel at the Woodley Park Zoo subway stop on Metro's Red Line. Run west on Woodley Road past the hotel. At 29th Street, stay on the road heading west past a small grassy section on the north side of the street. Run past a small wall with "Woodley" on it and up a small hill lined with houses. Cross Cleveland Avenue directly and run past the Belgian Embassy on the south side of the street. Run up a gentle hill to Massachusetts Avenue. You will run by the Greek Orthodox Cathedral at the corner of Massachusetts Avenue and Garfield Road. Turn right on Massachusetts Avenue and head northwest. On this part of the trail you will see the National Cathedral and its grounds.

Cross Wisconsin Avenue, keeping on the east side of Massachusetts Avenue. You will run down a long hill and then up a long gentle hill ending at Ward Circle. Run one-quarter of the way around Ward Circle (staying on the sidewalk, not crossing any street). You will then be heading northeast on Nebraska Avenue. You will run by the Naval Security Station and the local NBC station on your right. At the next light at Van Ness Street, turn right and run past the National Presbyterian Church and Center. Run down the small hill and up a slight grade to Wisconsin Avenue. Run past Wisconsin Avenue and down a slight grade crossing 38th Street and 37th Street. At the light at Reno Road, turn right (south). The sidewalk stops near the small traffic island at Upton Street and Reno Road. Continue south to the light at Tilden Street and turn left. Cross a small traffic island, staying either on the street or the worn path next to the street. Turn right on Segwick Street and run down a slight hill to Connecticut Avenue. Run south on Connecticut Avenue past a small shopping area, up a grade past the National Zoo, and down another grade to the starting point.

Special Information: This is a moderately rolling course run primarily on the sidewalk. On Connecticut Avenue there will be a considerable number of people. The rest of the course is less populated. Since this is not on a trail, there are few bicyclists to interfere, but watch for heavy auto traffic.

Dalecarlia Parkway

Location: Northwest Washington, southeast of the Dalecarlia Reservoir
Distance: 3.5   **Rating**: 2
Surface: Grass, sidewalk   **Population**: 2

    The Dalecarlia Parkway course is circular with a hidden attraction in the middle. You can start this run at Westmoreland Circle which is at the northwest border of the District of Columbia and Maryland.

    The best strategy is to run down the center of the parkway which is grassy and has a gentle downslope. At the bottom of the hill is the junction with Loughboro Road.

    Cross Loughboro to the other side (south) where the sidewalk is located, turn left (east), and run up the hill. For the most part, this is a considerable uphill run to the vicinity of American University. Cut to the north side of the street by American University to pick up the sidewalk. Turn left at Ward Circle and run northwest on the sidewalk which slopes downhill on Massachusetts Avenue. You will now be running back toward your point of origin. As you approach Westmoreland Circle, you will have to conquer one more uphill run.

    At the beginning of these directions, I said there was a hidden attraction on this course. The hidden attraction is Spring Valley, the neighborhood located in the center of the circular course. Spring Valley has some of the most beautiful homes in the Washington area. You will enjoy running some additional miles by taking side trips through the numerous streets throughout Spring Valley.

Special Information: The small shopping center at Massachusetts Avenue and Windom Street contains a filling station where you can buy soft drinks. Note that this course is not level, especially the run up Loughboro Street, but it is interesting. The majority of this course is on sidewalks.

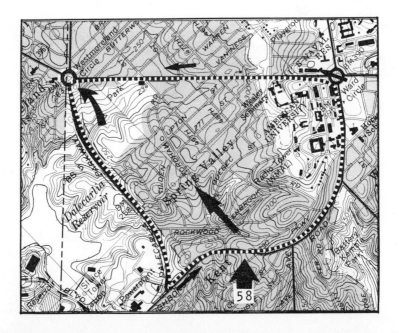

Southwest — Fort McNair

Location: Southwest Washington, southeast of the 14th Street Bridge
Distance: 4   **Rating**: 2
Surface: Grass, sidewalk   **Population**: 2

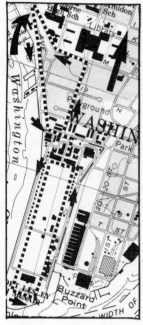

Park near Maine Avenue and 7th Street S.W. Begin running toward the waterfront, cross the waterfront access road behind the restaurants, and run north along the docks to the Yacht Club. Turn around and run back past where you started to the end of the walk. Continue along the fence and through the part by the Washington Channel to the boundary of Fort McNair.

At the end of the park next to the boundary with Fort McNair is the statue, "Titanic," erected by a group of American women in honor of the heroes of the SS Titanic. There is an annual event that is not well-known at this statue. A group of men raise glasses of champagne as a toast to those gentlemen who gave their lives on the Titanic so that others might live. This occurs each year on April 14, the anniversary of the sinking.

Turn left at the statue and work your way out to 4th and P Streets S.W. Continue straight ahead on P Street to the gate for Fort McNair. Turn right and enter the fort. Run straight ahead until you reach the parade ground. Because the fort is a part of the Military District of Washington, runners must wear shirts. Among other things, Fort McNair is famous as the site where the conspirators in the Lincoln assassination were executed. Turn right and follow the one-way street which circles the parade ground. Initially, you will pass officer housing, the Officers' Club, and the golf course. Run past the west side of the National War College, turn behind it, and run past the east side. Run north back toward the gate passing the Industrial College of the Armed Forces and the enlisted pool. Continue back to the main gate which is easy to find if you keep the parade ground on the inside. Return to the starting point by turning left on P Street, then right on 4th Street. Continue north on 4th Street to M Street S.W. Turn left (west) on M Street. As M Street goes around a bend, it becomes Maine Avenue. Continue on Maine Avenue to the point of origin. The entire course is extremely flat.
Special Information: This is a very pleasant run by the river, especially in the early evening. I do not recommend running this area at night.

Chapter 8
Maryland

The state of Maryland surrounds the Washington, D.C. area from the southeast to the northwest. There are numerous running trails throughout the state, but only those with relatively easy access to the Washington area will be discussed in this chapter.

The trails in Maryland range from some of the best to some of the worst. One of the best is the trail alongside MacArthur Boulevard which stretches from northwest Washington to Great Falls in Potomac, Maryland. Another excellent choice is the Sligo Creek Parkway Trail which runs to the vicinity of Wheaton Regional Park.

I found many interesting trails in Maryland more suitable for hiking than running. They were truly enjoyable, even though I often found myself hanging from cliffs, running through blackberry bushes, and fording streams.

There are other excellent Maryland trails not included in this chapter but described elsewhere in this book. Chapter 3 contains trails running through Montgomery County in Rock Creek Park. Chapter 5 details trails along the Potomac that are part of the C&O Canal Park. The Maryland trails in both these chapters are well maintained and excellent for running. Like Virginia, Maryland offers an interesting mix of rural and urban trails that should be popular with all runners and joggers.

Lower MacArthur Boulevard

Location: Montgomery County, just north of Washington, D.C. along the Potomac River

Distance: 5

Surface: Road, blacktop

Rating: 2

Population: 2

Park in the District of Columbia on MacArthur Boulevard just north of Loughboro Road. Run to the west side of the road and turn right (north). The property on both sides of the road in this area is owned by the Dalecarlia Reservoir. Run past the front of the waterworks on the sidewalk, cross into Maryland, and go around a bend and up a small hill. When you reach the top of the small hill, the sidewalk ends and you will have to run on the side of the road. Pass part of the Defense Mapping Agency on both sides of the road and an old gas station on the left. Start down a grade until you find a blacktopped path leading off to the left. Follow that path; it is the real beginning of the MacArthur Boulevard Trail. From this point to Glen Echo Park, the trail follows MacArthur Boulevard closely. It is long and level except for a small hill near the District of Columbia line.

Special Information: Glen Echo Park is now under the management of the National Park Service. Numerous artists and craftsmen exhibit their products here. In back of the parking lot at Glen Echo is the Clara Barton House which was built in 1897 and served as the headquarters of the American Red Cross until 1904. This is an easy trail to run with numerous trees on one side and a highway on the other. I marked it down in runnability because you must run on the road just north of the Washington, D.C. line.

Middle MacArthur Boulevard

Location: Montgomery County, in the vicinity of the Beltway along the Potomac River
Distance: 10
Surface: Blacktop

Rating: 1
Population: 2

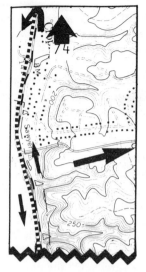

This section covers MacArthur Boulevard to Glen Echo Park from the parking lot of Old Anglers Inn.

The majority of this trail is on the side of MacArthur Boulevard. There are a number of major streets to cross but there is no serious problem with traffic except during rush hour. There are two short sections where you must run on the side of the road. In two instances the trail leaves the road and cuts away for a few hundred feet. At Glen Echo Park, it is possible to cut through the park and rejoin MacArthur Boulevard farther down on the other side of the park.

Special Information: There is no water available but there is a grocery store at Cabin John where refreshments can be obtained. You can run on the side of the trail on grass in many locations. There is not much shade available. I found this trail fun to run as you can really let go and open up.

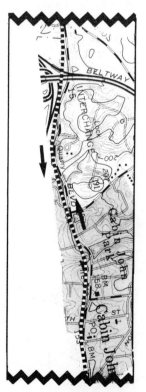

73

Upper MacArthur Boulevard

Location: Montgomery County, in the C&O Canal National Historical Park
Distance: 4.5   **Rating**: 2
Surface: Woods, trail   **Population**: 3

  Park at the north end of the parking lot at Great Falls. Run south to the Great
Falls Tavern which is now a museum. Just past the tavern you will come to another
trail leading off to the left and into the woods. The Appalachian Trail Club has
marked the trees along this route with blue blaze marks. Continue following these
marks for about 2-3/4 miles until you see yellow blaze marks on the left. Follow the
yellow markers which lead in the direction of the C&O Canal. The trail will end at
Berma Road. Follow this road to the left along the canal until you come to a gate
leading into the parking lot across from Old Anglers Inn. Return over the same
course.
Special Information: This trail can be run very easily, and yet it is deep in the
woods. The Great Falls Tavern has restrooms and water fountains available. This
trail is highly recommended, but it can be confusing because of the number of
cross-trails. On the day that I ran this trail, I passed a small group of deer about 2
miles into the woods.

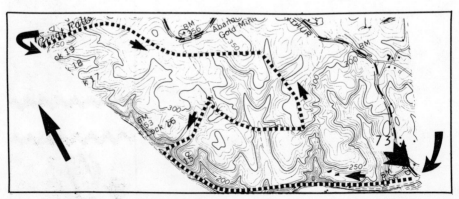

Little Falls Parkway

Location: Montgomery County, just north of the District line near the Potomac River
Distance: 4.5   **Rating**: 3
Surface: Blacktop, road   **Population**: 2

Park off Massachusetts Avenue, N.W., near Little Falls Parkway. Take the blacktop path south from Massachusetts Avenue; you can continue south on this path to Albermarle Street in Maryland. It does not go through to MacArthur Boulevard because of Dalecarlia Reservoir. There are a number of trees along this path and grass on which to run.

If you run north of Massachusetts Avenue, the trail is on the side of Little Falls Parkway which means heavy traffic. The traffic makes it difficult to cross at the light of River Road and Little Falls Parkway. If you cross over to Norway Street, you will see a sign welcoming you to the community of Somerset. Find the paved path leading north from this point on the east side which will take you into the park, away from the parkway. When the trail eventually branches, take the right branch up a hill to the east and exit on parkgrounds at Norwood Drive. Follow Norwood Drive to Wisconsin Avenue in Bethesda. Run north two blocks and turn left (west) on either Nottingham Street or Chevy Chase Street to Wellington Street. Turn south (left) on Wellington Street and run to the area where Wellington Street joins Little Falls Parkway. Continue running south and join the trail leading to Norwood Street.
Special Information: On the trail south of Massachusetts Avenue you will encounter a large number of people. The trail north of Massachusetts Avenue is dangerous because you must run alongside the parkway next to heavy traffic. The far north end of the trail is excellent, but it is too short to be run just for itself by the serious runner.

Sligo Creek Park, Piney Branch — Forest Glen

Location: Montgomery County, north of the District line and west of Prince Georges County

Distance: 4.4   **Rating**: 1

Surface: Blacktop   **Population**: 2

Park in the spaces located on the side of Sligo Creek Parkway near Piney Branch Road. The trail starts next to the parkway, cuts across a creek and through a playground. It then crosses back over the creek, runs behind a school, and continues north. Pass Wayne Avenue and then cross the creek on a small bridge. When you come to Colesville Road, there is a traffic light to help you cross without a problem. Continue running on the west side of the stream and through the grassy area under the Beltway. After running through the meadow, you will exit at Forest Glen Road.

Special Information: Although this trail runs close to the parkway, it maintains its separate identity because it follows the stream valley rather than the parkway. It is an easy running path, especially if you like to run on grass. If you are looking for a longer run, this trail can be combined with the next trail for a good 10-mile round trip run.

Sligo Creek Park, Forest Glen —Wheaton

Location: Montgomery County, east of the Beltway and
Georgia Avenue

Distance: 5.2   **Rating**: 1

Surface: Blacktop   **Population**: 2

Park on the streets near Forest Glen. Start running the
trail north from Forest Glen through the numerous trees.
Cross Dennis Avenue and continue along the west side of
the Sligo Creek Parkway. When the trail emerges on
University Boulevard, turn right, go over the bridge, and
then turn left on the north side of University Boulevard
where the bike path sign is located. Follow the bike path
into the middle of a wooded area, past a small shopping
area, and then back into the woods. The bike path
eventually turns left and continues west to Channing
Street. Run north along Channing Street past a
playground and turn left on Franwell Street. There is a
short blacktop path running north from here which
connects Blue Ridge Street, Arcola Avenue, and
Hermitage Street. The blacktop surface is in poor
conditions.

Special Information: Continuing north past Hermitage
Street you will enter the south side of Wheaton Regional
Park with its own set of trails. The northern part of this
trail through the woods is relatively free of people and
easy to run on. It is easier to run this trail along the side of
the blacktop.

Fort Washington

Location: Prince Georges County. Fort Washington can be reached via Maryland Route 210, Indian Head Highway, to Fort Washington Road. Follow Fort Washington Road to the park entrance.

Distance: 5

Surface: Grass, blacktop, dirt

Rating: 1

Population: 2

Park in the lot near the old fortress. Fort Washington was destroyed in 1814, rebuilt in 1824, and used during the Civil War. Run around the east side of the parking lot back to the entrance road. Run past the old parade grounds, turn down the first road on the right, proceed to the end of that road, and run across a meadow to Warburton Drive. Warburton Drive will take you to the picnic areas. Run to picnic area D and down a small hill to Battery Smith.

At the south end of Battery Smith, run down a steep hill to Piscataway Creek at the Potomac River. Turn right on the dirt path by the Potomac River. This is the River Trail. It is difficult to run initially because of roots and gullies; however, it soon becomes a good trail. Continue running to an old wagon trail. Take this trail to the base of the fortress by navigation light number 80. Proceed along the paved trail by the river to picnic area E. Continue onto a road, run the road one-quarter of the way up the hill and locate the service road on the left. Run the service road through the woods along the Potomac River and exit near the top of the hill by picnic area E2. Turn right and return to the parking lot.

Special Information: Fort Washington has water fountains and comfort stations everywhere. There are trees and woods along the Potomac River and considerable open space and picnic areas on top of the hill. This is a good place to get in whatever running mileage you desire.

Fort Foote

Location: Prince Georges County off the Beltway on the Potomac

Distance: 3

Surface: Dirt, grass

Rating: 3

Population: 3

Drive into Fort Foote on a graded dirt road. Park near the first parking spot on the left near the woods. Take the trail from here into the woods. Avoid the edge of the trail as it can be slippery. Notice the platforms for four siege guns dating from 1863 and still in place. Cross a small wooded bridge and take the rough trail to the right. You will run downhill to the stone beach on the Potomac River, come back up and take the trail to the left near the top of the hill, which will come out on the road. Continue running into Fort Foote and find a gentle trail at the end of the road. Run this trail to its end at the sandy beach on the Potomac River.

Just below this trail there is a paved access road that was closed on the day I ran it. After running through the park, I ran out to a large meadow near the park entrance, circled it, and returned to the car.

Special Information: I ran about 3 miles at Fort Foote. The park is not well maintained and there is no water. Comfort stations are primitive. This trail is satisfactory for jogging, but not recommended for running.

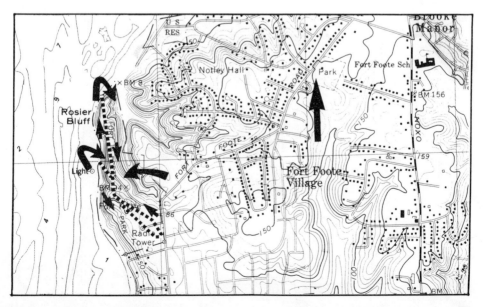

Cabin John Regional Park

Location: Montgomery County, northwest of Democracy Boulevard and the I-270 extension
Distance: 3.8   **Rating**: 2
Surface: Dirt, gravel, street   **Population**: 2

Park in the parking lot off Tuckerman Lane. Run west through the parking lot and right into the playground to begin the nature trail run. Run west to an access trail which intersects the nature trail. Run this access trail northwest to Tuckerman Lane. Cross Tuckerman Lane, run around a barrier and cross over Old Farm Creek on the small bridge. Continue running north along the access road which curves slowly to the right. Pass by the path on the left and continue running up a hill to the camping area. Run back down this same hill and take the side trail you passed previously. Run this trail north into the forest. This trail is only for jogging or hiking, not for running. The trail bends west when it exits the woods. Just at this exit, you will find a trail branching off to the left which connects with Mary Cassatt Street. Follow this street around as it bends from the south to the west and turn left on Seven Locks Road. Run Seven Locks Road south past the shopping center at Seven Locks Road and Tuckerman Lane. Run east on Tuckerman Lane on the north side of the street and cross back to the nature trail. Run the nature trail around to the south and west paralleling the miniature railroad. When the trail ends at the parking lot off Westlake Drive, cross the blacktop path just past the amphitheater to return to your starting point.

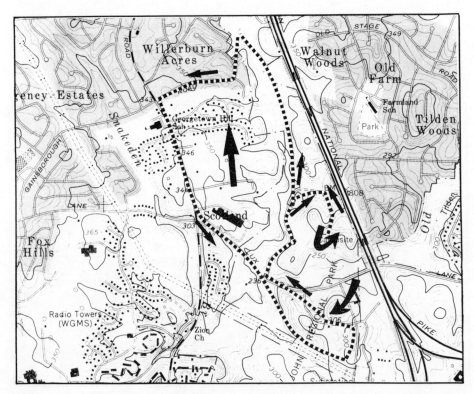

Wheaton Regional Park

Location: Montgomery County, northwest of University Boulevard and Georgia Avenue. To reach Wheaton Regional Park, turn right on Randolph Road from Georgia Avenue. Go two blocks to Glenallen Avenue which will bring you to the Nature Center parking lot.

Distance: 4

Surface: Crushed gravel, blacktop

Rating: 2

Population: 2

Park in the parking lot at the Brookside Nature Center in the park. Run to the southwest corner of the lot and turn right on the path toward the athletic area. Run past Pine Lake and across the miniature railroad tracks. Continue running past the brick pumping station and follow the paved trail back into the woods. Cross the paved north/south trail leading from Arcola Avenue. Stay along the outside edge of the park and remain on the primary trail. The secondary trails lead nowhere. The main trail will join a horse trail and pass near the stables before completing the circle back to the area of the nature center. Turn right to return to your starting point.

Special Information: This trail provides almost every type of terrain: nature trail, horse trail, blacktop, and meadow. When I ran this trail, I tried to stay to the outside of the park as much as possible. This led me to some secondary trails in the woods which became so faint that I could not tell where I was. There is water available at the athletic fields. When you finish your circular run, take the access trail from the Nature Center parking lot to Brookside Gardens. At Brookside Gardens there are both outdoor and indoor plants in the summer.

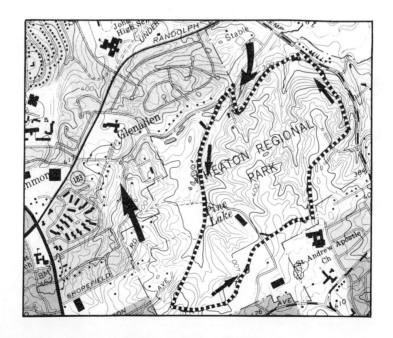

Location: Prince Georges County, beginning at the intersection of Bladensburg and Baltimore Roads east of the Anacostia River bridge on Bladensburg Road

Distance: 4.4   **Rating**: 2

Surface: Grass, blacktop   **Population**: 2

Park on Upshur Street at Bladensburg Road in the minipark at the Indian Queen Tavern. This small park is maintained by the Maryland National Capital Park and Planning Commission. Run south to Bladensburg Road and out to the flood control dike on the east side of the Anacostia River. Run north along the top of the dike and cross Baltimore Road and the Chessie System Railroad tracks. At Decatur Street, shift to the dike on the west side of the river and run north. At the approach to Riverdale Road, follow the path around an apartment building, cross Riverdale Road, and pick up the paved trail. Run under East-West Highway to Northeast Park just north of the highway. Return south over the same route except that when you reach Riverdale Road, cross the bridge to the east and run south on Tanglewood Drive. When you reach the south end of Tanglewood Drive, return to the dike and run back to Bladensburg Road.

Special Information: The Indian Queen Tavern was an inn during George Washington's time in 1752. The inn was built by Jacob Wirt before the Revolution when Bladensburg was a port town. Later, it was a stagecoach stop. Between 1774 and 1783, the inn was owned by Peter Carnes, a lawyer and balloonist. Carnes holds the distinction of making the first authenticated manned balloon ascent in America. This trail follows a worn path on top of the dikes. North of College Park, the trail is paved and is great for running. Details are given in the next section.

Anacostia River, NE Branch, North Half

Location: Prince Georges County, west of Kenilworth Avenue and east of downtown College Park
Distance: 5.5   **Rating**: 1
Surface: Blacktop   **Population**: 2

Park in the lot on the south side of Calvert Street just east of the Northeast Branch. A relatively new par course exercise trail begins at the Calvert Street Park. Run south along the Dennis Wolf trail to just north of the East-West Highway. Water is available in the comfort station on the southwest corner of the park.

Turn here and run north past where you parked. Run under Calvert Street north past the back of the runway at the College Park Airport. Continue north, enter Paint Branch Park and cross a small bridge over Paint Branch. Follow the trail along the west side of Indian Creek to a point where the trail runs straight ahead and a bridge is on the right. Take the bridge to the right or you will end up on a connector trail to the University of Maryland which is covered in another section. Cross Berwyn Street and take the trail turning right to exit on 57th Street and Greenbelt Road (University Boulevard). There are service stations in the area where you can get refreshments. Return over the same trail.

Special Information: Since the trail is flat with few interruptions, it is excellent for building up your running speed. It is a well-marked trail and has my. highest recommendation. The parks are closed after dark.

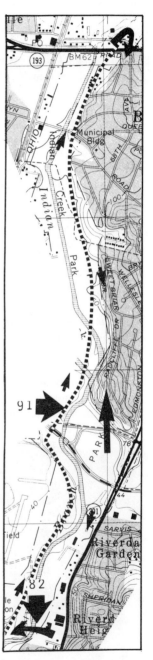

Anacostia River, NW Branch
Riggs Road — Rhode Island Avenue

Location: Prince Georges County, at Riggs Road near the University of Maryland
Distance: 8.4   **Rating**: 3
Surface: Blacktop, dirt, grass   **Population**: 2

Park at Old Adelphi Mill on Riggs Road and start running south from the parking lot. Cross the Northwest Branch by wading through a ford. At best this is a summer or spring only trail. After crossing the river you will come to another parking lot. This lot can be reached via West Park Drive and is probably a more reasonable starting point. Continue running across University Boulevard to the park on the south side. This is the end of the paved trail. Run along the west side of the park, crossing bridges back and forth over the Northwest branch. Be sure to end up on the west side. The east side of the river is not runnable beyond this point. Locate the marker for the gas pipe line right-of-way and follow that right-of-way south past a playground and exit along East-West Highway. Cross the bridge to the east side of the Northwest Branch on East-West Highway. Step over the guardrail and run through a large meadow along the Northwest Branch. Stay close to the stream and cross over a footbridge to the west side. Turn left (southeast) on Ager Road and run to Queens Chapel Road. Both sides of the river south of Ager Road are difficult to run. On Queens Chapel Road cross to the west side of the Northwest Branch. Run southeast along the stream behind some housing units. Where 37th Street meets the Northwest Branch, the Corps of Engineers has built a high flood control dike. You can easily run the top of this dike to Rhode Island Avenue. This part of the trail is the only good part other than the paved start. Stop at Rhode Island Avenue, as it is impossible to cross the Chessie System railroad tracks. Return over the same course.

Special Information: There are numerous ditches to cross, and some swamps which can present problems when it has been raining. This is more of a cross-country trail for hiking rather than a running or jogging trail. The south end of the dike offers no shade.

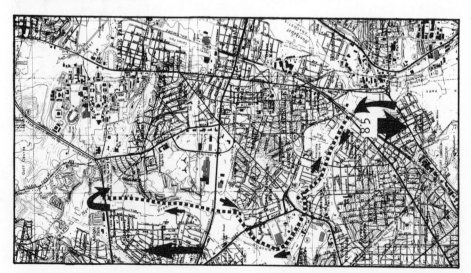

Anacostia River, NW Branch, Riggs Road — Oak View

Location: Prince Georges and Montgomery Counties. Riggs Road north of University Boulevard and west of the University of Maryland

Distance: 4

Surface: Blacktop

Rating: 2

Population: 2

Park at the parking lot at the Old Adelphi Mill. Run north over a small footbridge and pass under the bridges at New Hampshire Avenue and Piney Branch Road. Next, ford a small stream and at the end of the paved trail, find the dirt trail that enters from the right (east). Run along this trail to the top of the long hill and exit on Oak View Drive.

Special Information: You will find numerous runners from the University of Maryland along with bicyclists and fishermen on this trail. The Old Adelphi Mill was built in 1796 and ceased operations as a grist mill in the middle of the last century.

Anacostia River, NW Branch, Oak View Drive
Colesville Road

Location: Montgomery County, between Colesville Road and the Beltway
Distance: 2.5
Surface: Dirt path

Rating: 3+
Population: 3

Park near the NW Branch on Oak View Drive. You can run north from Oak View Drive only with difficulty. The trail from Oak View Drive to the Beltway is actually better for hiking. It is possible to run north from the Beltway; however, it is a very rough trail. (It is also the trail where I twisted my ankle.) You will also have to leap across several small streams until you come to a gravel trail going up a hill. Jog this trail, although it is impossible to keep going straight as you will run into a large number of huge rocks. The trail climbs to a high peak overlooking the river. Exit the trail behind a filling station near the Washington Suburban Sanitary Commission.

Special Information: I do not recommend this as a running trail even though it can be jogged on the east side of the river. Do not even attempt this trail on the west side.

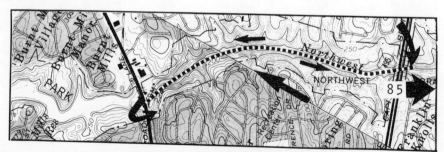

Greenbelt Park Road

Location: Prince Georges County, east of Kenilworth Avenue, and north of Riverdale Road (East-West Highway)

Distance: 4.2   **Rating**: 1

Surface: Road   **Population**: 2

Park along Good Luck Road on the south side of Greenbelt Park. Run from the small parking area north up a hill on Park Central Road. At the top of the hill there is a traffic barrier. Run to the left around the barrier on a short trail and return to Park Central Road on the other side of the barrier. Continue running north on Park Central Road passing the Dogwood Nature Trail and turn right on the road immediately beyond the nature trail. This road takes you in a large circle back to the Park Central Road only running south. Continue back to your starting point.

Special Information: Since there is a barrier on the primary north/south road, traffic is at a minimum. There is little impediment to a fast run. This park contains picnic and camping facilities and water at some of the picnic areas. Greenbelt Park is under the control of the National Park Service. The park includes 1,100 acres. You will see only a small part of this acreage on the main road so I have included two additional trails to cover more of the park.

Special Note: Maps for all three Greenbelt Park trails may be found on the following page.

Greenbelt Park, Nature Trails

Location: Prince Georges County, east of Kenilworth Avenue, and north of Riverdale Road (East-West Highway)

Distance: 3.8   **Rating**: 2

Surface: Dirt   **Population**: 3

The Park Service maintains three circular nature trails at Greenbelt Park. They are: the Azalea Trail, the Blueberry Trail, and the Dogwood Trail. Each of these trails is well marked and easy to follow, so I have not detailed a particular course. The Azalea and Blueberry Trails are each 1.2 miles long. The Dogwood Trail is 1.4 miles long. These tails have a common problem which runners should beware of, i.e., many hidden roots and branches on which a runner can trip or turn an ankle. The Azalea Trail circles a lovely large meadow which you can run through if you become tired of running through the woods.

Special Information: There are benches located in the woods for use by runners, joggers, and hikers. There is water available at the comfort station near the parking lot across from the entrance at Greenbelt Road.

You may want to consider running these trails in association with the other two trails in Greenbelt Park if you want additional distance.

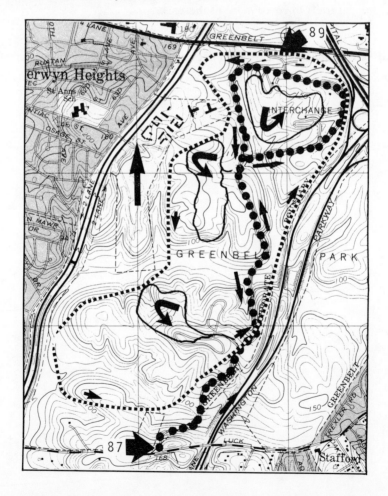

Greenbelt Park, Horse and Hiking Trails

Location: Prince Georges County. Enter on Greenbelt Road (East-West Highway) just east of Kenilworth Avenue (Maryland Route 201)

Distance: 6   **Rating**: 2

Surface: Dirt   **Population**: 3

    Start near the north entrance to Greenbelt Park. The trail is well marked where it crosses the access road to the park. If you run the trail counterclockwise, you will circle the park passing within view of the highrises near Kenilworth Avenue. This trail includes part of the Blueberry Trail discussed in the previous section of this book. Continue running the trail toward the southwest part of the park going past a campground. Run uphill crossing the Park Central Road near the vehicle barrier. Follow the trail along the east side of the roadway back toward your starting point.

    Special Information: Horse trails are not particularly good for running because of unevenness from hoof prints and the obvious problem of horse droppings. This trail is closed at dark.

Special Note: A map for all three Greenbelt Park trails may be found on the preceding page.

Suitland Parkway

Location: Prince Georges County, along the Suitland Parkway, 3-1/2 miles east of the District/Maryland line

Distance: 6.6   **Rating**: 3

Surface: Stones, dirt   **Population**: 2

Park on the parallel access road west of Suitland Road on the north side of the Suitland Parkway. This access road doubles as a park. Run east across the Suitland Road access road and over the bridge across Suitland Road. Pass another small bridge and run east along the parkway. As you reach Forestville Road, the trail leads north a short distance away from the parkway. As you run under the Beltway you will find that the trail deteriorates and becomes a small rough path. Eventually, you will reach Old Marlboro Pike north of Andrews Air Force Base.

Special Information: I dislike this trail from a safety standpoint. You are alone along a highway without many other runners around. The trail is dull with a busy highway on one side and a thick wall of bushes and trees on the other. Also, the trail is rough, not well maintained, and lacks shade and water. I have included this trail because it is highly visible from the road, and, as a result, many people are curious about it.

Anacostia, NE Branch — University of Maryland

Location: Prince Georges County, east of the University of Maryland and west of the Anacostia NE Branch Trail
Distance: 3.5
Surface: Blacktop, road, sidewalk

Rating: 2
Population: 2

Park on the south side of Calvert Road and run under the road north past the College Park Airport. Run along the west side of Indian Creek. Where the bridge crosses west over Indian Creek, continue running north.

The paved trail continues on for a short distance and exits onto Cleveland Avenue. Run northwest on Cleveland Avenue on the side of the street. Turn right and run north to Lakeland Road. Run Lakeland Road west over the railroad crossing and continue west along the south side of Lakeland road on the sidewalk to Lakeland Park. Run through the park on a blacktop trail staying to the north side of the park. Continue running west through the small woods to emerge on the sidewalk along Lakeland Road. Lakeland Road deadends at Washington Baltimore Boulevard (U.S. 1) on the northeast corner of the campus of the University of Maryland. Run south on the sidewalk along U.S. 1 one block to Campus Lane, one of the primary entrances to the University of Maryland. Continue running south to Calvert Road. Turn east, running along the north side of the street. Once outside of the city, cross the street to the south side and continue running west to your point of origin.

Special Information: I view this trail mainly as a connection link with the Anacostia River NE Branch Trail. Lakeland Park is nice, but its size offers nothing out of the ordinary for running or jogging. There is a circular exercise trail in Lakeland Park.

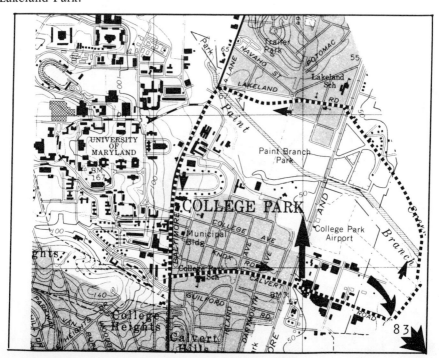

Columbia, Town Center

Location: Howard County, Maryland; Columbia is located off U.S. 29 west of Maryland Route 175, approximately 28 miles north of downtown Washington
Distance: 2.4 **Rating**: 2
Surface: Blacktop, sidewalk, road **Population**: 2

    At the Town Center of Columbia, park on the south side of Columbia Mall. Proceed to the southeast corner of the mall and turn east along the mall access road on the south side. At this point, you will be running on the side of the street. The street deadends on the Little Patuxent Parkway. Run south on the parkway on a blacktop trail which bends quickly around to the west. Continue running on the blacktop trail when the Little Patuxent Parkway meets the Governor Warfield Parkway leading north. Run north on the trail beside the Governor Warfield Parkway over some small gentle hills. Run past a small woods on your left. At the first street that you come to, run south on the north access to the mall. The blacktop trail ends at this point. Run south on the sidewalk which ends when the road bends to the right. Run on the edge of the road around the mall to your starting point.

    Special Information: This trail is not overly exciting, but it does serve as a general orientation tour to downtown Columbia. To complete a running orientation of downtown Columbia, you should run the Lake Kittamaqundi path described on the previous page of this book.

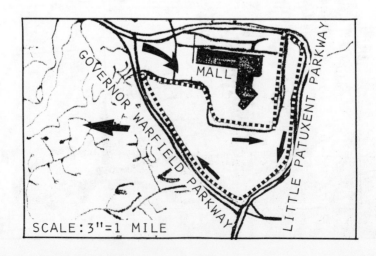

SCALE: 3"=1 MILE

Columbia, Lake Kittamaqundi

Location: Howard County; Town Center, Columbia, Maryland
Distance: 3.4
Surface: Blacktop, sidewalk

Rating: 2
Population: 1

Park on the east side of Town Center near the Twin Cinemas and the Exhibit Center. Run down a series of steps to the edge of Lake Kittemaqundi. Run north behind the shops and restaurants where the trail becomes a blacktop surface. Run to the northwest and cross a small stream that connects Lake Kittemaqundi and Wilde Lake. Running into some woods, you will find par course exercise stations on each side of the trail. The trail exits on the east side of the Little Patuxent Parkway. Run to the next corner, turn right, and run the sidewalk up a small hill. When the road bends to the right around Vantage Point Road, stay on the sidewalk, do not run the road up to Oakland Manor. Run Vantage Point Road to the cul-de-sac and reverse your course to your point of origin. Once your reach Town Center, continue south along the blacktop trail on the southwest side of Lake Kittamaqundi. When you reach the south end of the lake, the trail turns east and crosses over the Little Patuxent River and U.S. 29. The pedestrian bridge contains more graffiti than any other single object in the greater Washington area. The trail winds past some apartments and up a hill to Steven's Forest Road in the Village of Oakland Mills. Return over the same trail to Town Center.

Special Information: I was disappointed to find that a trail did not totally circle Lake Kittamaqundi. This is a good trail to run if you want to be around people. There are also numerous places to get refreshments downtown when you are hot and sweaty.

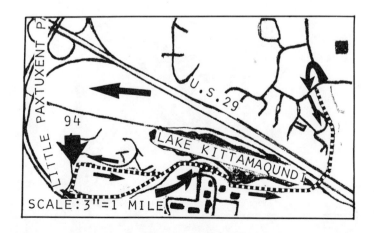

Columbia, Wilde Lake

Location: Howard County, Maryland; Town Center, Columbia, Maryland
Distance: 2.2   **Rating**: 2
Surface: Blacktop, sidewalk   **Population**: 1

Park on the east side of Town Center near the Twin Cinemas and the Exhibit Center. Run north along the lake and then northwest past the par course exercise trail along the blacktop path leading to Little Patuxent Parkway. At the corner of Hyla Brook Road, turn left and run across Little Patuxent Parkway into Wilde Lake Park. When you reach a trail branching to the left, turn left and run down a slight hill and cross the small bridge at the bottom. Notice on your right that the dam for Wilde Lake is composed of artificial logs. Run up the hill to dam level and then southwest along Wilde Lake behind the backs of the townhouses along the lake. The path leaves the lake at the Cove development. Run out the Cove and then northwest on the sidewalk along Governor Warfield Parkway back to Hyla Brook Road. Return to your starting place over the same trail.

Special Information: Wilde Lake has no path that totally circles the lakes. As in some locations, the townhouses come all the way down to the Lake. This path can be combined with Lake Kittamaqundi to provide a longer run.

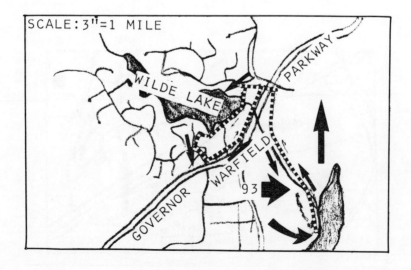

Columbia, Lake Elkhorn

Location: Howard County; Village of Owen Brown, Columbia. Go east on MD 175 3.3 miles from U.S. 29. Turn right and go 2.4 miles on Snowden River Parkway. Turn right where the parkway deadends on Broken Land Parkway, proceed north one-half mile to Cradlerock Way. Go east 0.2 miles to Swan Point.

Distance: 1.18
Surface: Blacktop

Rating: 1
Population: 1

    Park near Swan Point, just off Cradlerock Way. Begin running near Swan Point on the north side of Lake Elkhorn and run clockwise around the lake. This path has more open space than the other lakes in Columbia and it completely circles the lake. Run east on the trail along the north side of the lake past small trees and behind two sets of townhouses. The trail branches at the east end of the lake. One branch continues east and is really an access trail that starts in the east at Sylvan Dell Court. Take the right branch which goes over a small stream on a wooden bridge. Once over the bridge, locate another access trail which joins the Lake Elkhorn Trail from the southeast. Stay on the lakeside trail and you will be on the correct path. The trail rises on a small hill and then falls back to the lake level. When you reach the west end of the trail, pass behind the dam in view of a pleasantly designed dam and spillway. Continue around the end of the lake and start running back east. Run past a small clock and around a bend to return to your starting point.

    Special Information: Although this trail is not very long, it is a very pleasant run and highly recommended. The path is made for running. If you want more distance, just keep circling the lake. I did not see any available water, so if you are going for a long run, you should take your own.

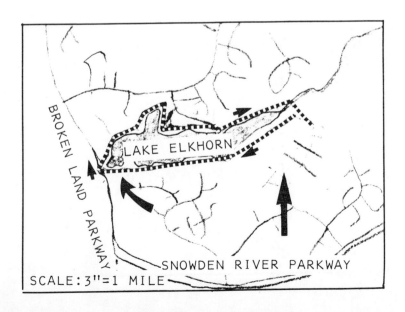

Chapter 9
Virginia

Virginia offers an exciting mix of urban and rural trails which are, for the most part, well maintained and excellent for running, biking, and hiking. When combined with the fact that these trails are often highly accessible, they can also be highly congested. Two major trail systems in Virginia have been given separate chapters. They are: Chapter 4, The Mount Vernon Parkway Trails, and Chapter 6, The W&OD Trails.

Trails discussed in this chapter include Burke Lake Trail, an outstanding trail through quiet woods overlooking Burke Lake; Four-Mile Run Trail, a topographically diverse run through residential Alexandria and quiet rolling woodlands; the Reston Trails, five enjoyable trails through one of America's premier planned "new towns"; and Zachary Taylor-Marcey Road Park, a short, almost-wilderness run, in close-in Arlington.

The District of Columbia is known for historic sites, but Northern Virginia has its share as well. Mount Vernon, Old Town, Arlington Cemetery, and the Pentagon are among the better known sites in Virginia. As you run the Virginia trails, you will encounter other equally well known, and many lesser known sites, important to America and its history.

Because of the variety of trails, changes in topography, and the historic nature of the area, Virginia trails can offer challenge and interest to all runners. The trails in this chapter, along with those in Chapter 4 and Chapter 6, will give you an excellent introduction to running in the Northern Virginia area.

Zachary Taylor — Marcey Road Park

Location: Arlington County, Virginia, north of Lee Highway and south of Glebe Road
Distance: 3.5   **Rating**: 1
Surface: Crushed gravel, road   **Population**: 2

Park near Military Road and 31st Street in Arlington. Run south on Military Road to the bottom of the hill where Donaldson Run crosses the road. Turn right and start on the trail running southwest up a long gentle grade. The trail crosses the stream twice on the way up the hill. The first part of this trail exits near Vernon and Upton Streets. Cross Vernon and turn right as the trail continues up the hill and increases in steepness.

The trail exits on 26th Street near Glebe Road not too far from Marymount College. If you enjoy running hills, you will find this a great trail of smooth crushed gravel. Return to Military Road over the same route.

Turn right on Military Road and run one block south. Cross Military Road and run northeast on Marcey Road. Enter Marcey Road Park and run past the parking lot. There are gravel-covered side trails entering from the right. Pass two houses, one on each side, and a park building. The pavement ends at a dirt trail. At this point, you should stop and return. I continued down the hill and ended up along the George Washington Parkway, but it is really impossible to run down to this point. I came back up the hill and tried to run down one of the side trails, but it was also impossible to run on these, as the terrain was just too steep. Run out of the park and return to your point of origin.

Special Information: I enjoyed the run from Military Road to 26th Street more than the run in Marcey Road Park. However, if you want to run over more mileage, Marcey Road Park is fine.

Location: Arlington County, Virginia, between I-66 and Walter Reed Drive.

Distance: 6.0   **Rating**: 1

Surface: Blacktop   **Population**: 2

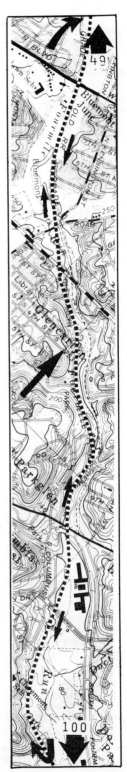

This part of the Four-Mile Run Trail runs from I-66 to Walter Reed Drive. The trail branches from the Martha Custis Trail by I-66 near Patrick Henry Drive (Bon Air Park). There are two joining points with small footbridges crossing Four-Mile Run from the Custis Trail. If you are running west on the Custis Trail, look for the sign saying John Marshall Bike Path; if you are running east, a sign specifies "Four-Mile Run Trail." From the Custis Trail to Walter Reed Drive, the trail is a pleasure to run; it passes through woods and has a rolling contour. It cuts under major roads and is primarily blacktop with spots of packed crushed gravel. The Arlington Park System has erected shelters along this trail. At points, the trail becomes confusing within the parks because of the numerous trails throughout this area. The best advice is to follow Four-Mile Run as closely as possible and follow the Bike Path signs. I ran this on a weekend and it was not crowded with runners or bicyclists.

Special Information: This is a great trail to run. I thoroughly enjoyed the considerable shade, changing contours, and lack of a multitude of runners and bicyclists. There is no water supply convenient to the trail.

Location: Arlington and Alexandria, Virginia, in the vicinity of National Airport

Distance: 6.2   **Rating**: 2

Surface: Blacktop, sidewalk   **Population**: 2

This part of the Four-Mile Run Trail includes the Anderson Bikeway and runs from Walter Reed Drive to the Mount Vernon Trail. Run Walter Reed Drive east along the south side of Arlington Mill Drive to Randolph Drive where the Four-Mile Run Trail actually stops. Run through Shirlington via Randolph Drive/28th Street to the footbridge over I-395 (Shirley Highway).

After crossing I-395, run along Gunston Road to Martha Custis Drive. Run east on Martha Custis Drive to east Glebe Road and then west on East Glebe Road to Four-Mile Run. Go across the bridge over East Glebe Road. Pick up the Anderson Bikeway on the south side of Glebe Road, and continue running east until the bikeway ends at Arlington County's advanced wastewater treatment plant. Run south on the sidewalk past the plant until you reach Jefferson Davis Highway. Locate a sign pointing to the Mount Vernon Trail. Run down a ramp from the sign to the west. You will soon double back and pass under the railyard. Join the Mount Vernon Trail just south of the south parking lot at National Airport.

If you run from the other direction and need to locate this trail from the Mount Vernon Trail, watch carefully for the turnoff, which is not well marked. The Mount Vernon Trail goes to the west while the access to the tunnel for Four-Mile Run is to the east, just south of the south airport parking lot. If there is any confusion, especially around Shirlington with its busy streets, follow the signs.

Special Information: This entirely paved trail is generally unshaded and out in the open. It is a hot run in the summertime. It gives a profound view of the working and smells of a sewage treatment plant. There is no water available near the trail. You will pass near a Seven-Eleven on East Glebe Road.

Holmes Run III Park

Location: 10 miles west of D.C., in Fairfax County near Seven Corners
Distance: 4.0 **Rating**: 2
Surface: Crushed gravel, blacktop **Population**: 3

Park near Hockett Street on a dirt area located just off Annandale Road or at Roundtree Park east of Hockett Street. Roundtree Park has a paved parking area, picnic facilities, restrooms, a water fountain, a baseball field at the rear of the park, and a path which leads to the Holmes Run III Park Trail. After running down the trail from Hockett Street, you can continue down a footpath straight along the stream or follow the main trail which loops back up toward Roundtree Park but stays in the woods. On the footpath, the trail is crushed stone. Eventually, you will pass an electric substation near Rose Lane, a street which opens onto the park on the north. Stay on the north side of the stream even though a small bridge crosses the stream near the substation. Later you will cross the stream on cut-off cement piles. Run up a hill and exit the park on Sprucedale Drive.

It is possible to run four miles in this park by exploring all the access routes into the park and the various paths. If you run the entire length, the best way back is to run back over the eastern half of the course. In the middle of the course, you can run one way along the stream and then reverse your route on the north leg near Roundtree Park.

Special Information: The majority of the trail consists of crushed stone with certain asphalt-paved areas. There is no space for running on grass along the trail, but there is considerable shade as most of the path is through the woods. This is an easy running trail. I enjoyed the section which looped toward Roundtree Park. I ran this trail during a weekday in May and met only two sets of hikers.

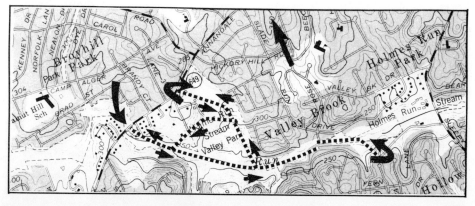

Mason District Park

Location: 2.8 miles west of Baileys Crossroads
Distance: 1
Surface: Crushed gravel

Rating: 1
Population: 1

Park on the south side of Columbia Pike just below the trail. After leaving the parking lot, run southwest up a small grade. The trail is a fairly level crushed gravel, circular par course. If you follow the exercise stations on the trail, you will run approximately one mile. In early June 1984, a construction company was in the process of building an outdoor amphitheater which may provide hazards or inconveniences in the future.

Special Information: This course has an equal amount of shade and sun. The start of the path is in the open; the back half is under trees. I met ten runners and walkers on this course on a midweek afternoon.

If you study a map before you run in the Annandale area, you can run Luria Park, Holmes Run III Park, and Mason District Park, all of which are connected by local streets. The entire run between these parks can be 9 to 10 miles, depending on the roads selected. Runners must be careful when running on major, heavily traveled streets in this area, such as Annandale Road or Gallows Road. These roads are hilly in places with no sidewalks and provide poor visibility for runners and drivers.

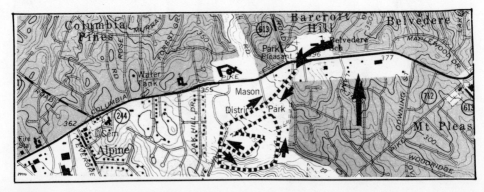

Holmes Run, Cameron Station — Potomac River

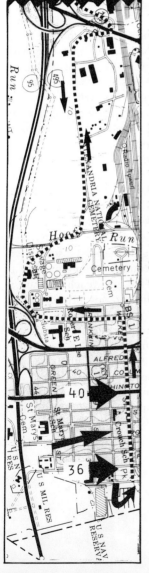

Location: Alexandria, Virginia, between Cameron Station and the Potomac River
Distance: 9.2   **Rating**: 1
Surface: Blacktop, road   **Population**: 2

Park at Cameron Run Regional Park or at Jordan Street and Holmes Run Parkway just off Duke Street in Alexandria. Start running at Duke Street along the northeast side of Holmes Run. After running under two railroad bridges, the trail emerges by Cameron Run Regional Park. Continue running along Holmes Run on a paved path following the many bike path signs. Run along Frontage Road, where there is a smell of honeysuckle in the spring, onto Mill Road. Turn south and run past the front of the Hoffman Building. Follow Eisenhower Avenue east past the Hoffman parking lot and the Eisenhower Yellow Line Metro stop. Continue running to the end of Eisenhower Avenue on the sidewalk.

When you come to the Alexandria and Fairfax County Wastewater Treatment Plant fence, run east between the plant and I-95. You will be aware of a strong sewage smell. Bend around the cloverleaf and run past the Alexandria Animal Shelter up Payne Avenue (north) to Wilkes Street where Payne Street deadends. Run east on Wilkes Street, across Henry and Patrick Streets, over the concrete access road between some townhouses, and then back to Wilkes and Fairfax Streets. Run through a big tunnel to deadend with the Mount Vernon Trail and the Potomac River at Union Street. Return over the same route.

Special Information: This trail is easy to run but not very exciting. It is paved its entire distance, but there is no shade or water.

Holmes Run, Cameron Station — Fairfax County Line

Location: Alexandria, Virginia—Cameron Station north to the Fairfax County Line
Distance: 4.5
Surface: Blacktop, crushed gravel

Rating: 2
Population: 2

Park just south of Duke Street off Jordan Street and Holmes Run Parkway and run north around the parking lot of an apartment complex. Cross Duke Street at an intersection on the north side and run west one block to a filling station. Locate a sign pointing to Brook Valley Regional Park. Pick up the blacktopped trail with numerous exercise stations along the way. This trail is actually designated as a jogging trail; there is considerable room to run on the grass. Near Paxton Street, the trail becomes packed cinders but there is grass on the side. Just short of the I-395 underpass, you will have to choose which one of two designated bike paths to follow. I chose the designated scenic path to the left versus the urban path over city streets proceeding to the right.

If you choose to run the scenic route, you will have to ford Holmes Run. At usual water level, you can cross over the rocks below the ford without getting wet, but use extreme care. Follow the concrete paved portion on the southwest side of the trail running north. Pass under Van Dorn Street, then through a large corrugated pipe under I-395. This can be wet in places. When you come out, you will be running on an evenly crushed stone path through the woods. Next, cross to the east side of the stream over a dry ford and continue north along the northeast side where the trail is concrete. The trail changes from concrete to crushed gravel in this section. When you reach the park at the Fairfax County line, you can't go any further on the east side. I backtracked and ran over a mulched trail north away from Holmes Run just before the end of the trail. The trail ends at the Ramsey Nature Center, 5700 Sanger Road. There is a circular trail there through the woods with a number of observation posts.

Special Information: This is an excellent running path except for the difficulties encountered in crossing Holmes Run.

Holmes Run, Fairfax County Line — Columbia Pike

Location: Fairfax County, Virginia, near Columbia and Leesburg Pikes
Distance: 1.25   **Rating**: 3+
Surface: Dirt, boulders   **Population**: 3

This part of the Holmes Run Trail is not recommended for normal running, but if you are a nature lover and insist, it is passable. As you run the trail north to the Fairfax County line, it becomes impossible to run further on the east side of Holmes Run because of a fence and the steep bank. At the Ramsey Nature Center described in the preceding section, it is possible during low water to ford the stream at the center's observation post 13. Follow the edge of the bank of Holmes Run to avoid a private club on the west side. You will soon enter some woods with numerous access paths down to the stream. If your destination is north, before Columbia Pike find an access path across Holmes Run to the northeast side. When you reach Columbia Pike, return over the same course.

Special Information: Remember, this is not a real running trail as there are too many hazards and private property to circumvent. It is impossible to go farther north on Holmes Run even though this trail is only one and one-quarter miles long. When I ran through this section, I decided to continue west along Columbia Pike to Mason District Park in Annandale and run the par course there.

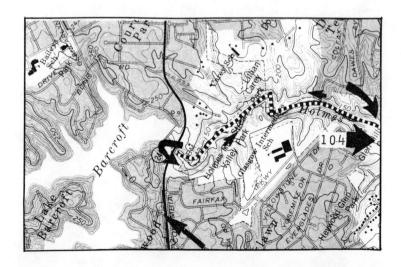

New Four-Mile Run Trail

Location: Arlington County, just north of Alexandria
Distance: 3.0   **Rating**: 1
Surface: Blacktop   **Population**: 2

   This trail follows the north side of Four-Mile Run Drive in Arlington. The trail starts just west of the Shirley Highway near the north side of the Shirlington exit.

   This trail runs under electric high-tension lines. It is a blacktopped trail running along the grass right-of-way in an area designated as Four-Mile Run Park. The trail runs northwest to Columbia Pike with a slight upgrade toward Columbia Pike. It is a relatively short trail with stop signs for cross-streets. To return, follow the same trail back.

Special Information: Running the long-distance Four-Mile Run Trail means running south of Four-Mile Run Drive and winding through the woods. If you do not want to run through the woods, or if you want to run in the evenings, this is a good trail.

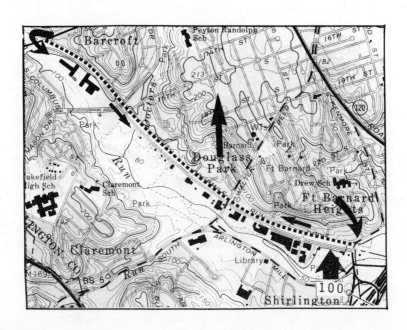

Pentagon — South 23rd Street

Location: The Pentagon and South Arlington
Distance: 5.2 **Rating**: 2
Surface: Blacktop **Population**: 2

Park in the visitors' parking area on Channel Drive and begin running from Pentagon North Parking to the freeway leading to Memorial Bridge. Run up the small hill and then south along the freeway past the west side of the Pentagon. Turn to the left when you pass the south corner of the Pentagon and run to the middle of South Parking turning right at the crosswalk and then up the center walkway toward I-395. At the edge of the parking lot, locate the crosswalk to the tunnel under I-395, cross the street, and enter the tunnel. When you come out of the tunnel, cross the parking lot, run to Army Navy Drive, turn right and cross the street at the light. Continue west on Army Navy Drive, running up the hill. As you come down the hill, the sidewalk ends for a few hundred yards. Run under Ridge Road and continue along Army Navy Drive. Shortly after the overpass, a blacktop trail reappears along the east side of the road. Continue to South 23rd Street, turn left and run up the hill. Cross Ridge Road at the light and run down the hill on South 23rd Street. At the base of the hill, turn left on Joyce Street and follow the street to a small park on your right. Run along the edge of the park until you reach Army Navy Drive. Turn right and return to the tunnel entrance and follow the route back to your car.

Special Information: This is a run with two challenging hills that offer a distinct change of pace from the flat Potomac River Trails in the vicinity of the Pentagon.

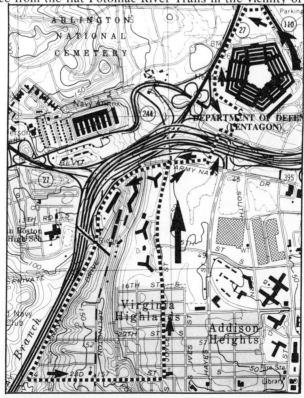

Burke Lake Park

Location: 23 miles southwest of Washington, D.C. From the Beltway (I-495) take Braddock Road west 1.8 miles to Burke Lake Road, turn left, and go 4.8 miles, turn left on Ox Road. After 0.6 miles, turn left into the park

Distance: 5.1   **Rating**: 1

Surface: Crushed gravel   **Population**: 2

Start at the Burke Lake Marina and run north on a crushed gravel course with considerable shade. The trail circles the lake and keeps it in view for most of the course. The par course is one of the best exercise courses in the greater metropolitan area; there is considerable room to run between each station. Near the southwest corner of the lake, look for a sign with fishing information. Just north of this sign, you can decide whether to run near the lake or stay on the crushed gravel path.

This is an excellent trail which you can run at top speed.

Special Information: I passed one bicyclist and a number of hikers. I located two drinking fountains in the park. During the summer, the snack bar at the marina will be open. There are restrooms just inside the looped drive in the park. On weekends and holidays there is a $3.50 charge for automobiles not registered in Fairfax County to enter the park. The park closes at dark.

Burke Lake Park was originally acquired by the FAA for an airport after World War II. When the airport was not constructed, the land was turned over to the County Park Authority.

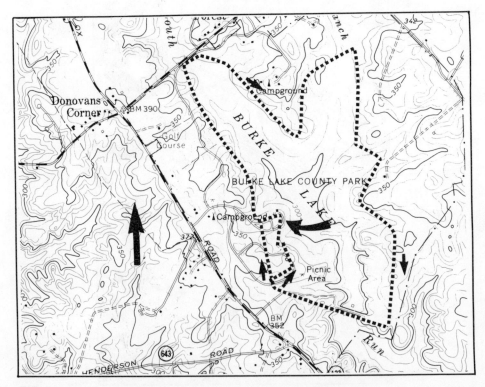

Lake Accotink

Location: Fairfax County, Virginia, south of Braddock Road and west of Springfield
Distance: 4   **Rating**: 2
Surface: Blacktop, gravel   **Population**: 2

Drive to the north parking lot at Accotink Park via Queensberry Avenue and Heming Avenue. Start at the far end of the parking lot and run down a blacktopped trail staying to the west of the parking lot and marina. Cross the paved road and stay to the left. The trail soon turns to gravel. Cross the spillway, if not at high water. In this section the trail is very level and straight. It goes up a short hill and curves through the woods to emerge eventually on a long straightaway with a fence along the outside. Just as the trail turns to the left, there is a small blacktopped trail entering on the right. Take this trail and run down a small hill to Danbury Forest Drive past Kings Glen School. Run past the school until you come to a trail at an angle from the street. Go down the steps and run over a small bridge turning right on a gravel trail paralleling a small creek. You will end up running along a paved trail near some homes and will soon emerge along a Perrier par course. Run across a small canal, then between the snack bar and the carrousel. Jog a slope to the right of the playground which will lead you to a paved trail and parking lot.
Special Information: There is a water fountain and restrooms at the snack bar. This was a rather dull run with a poor view of the lake.

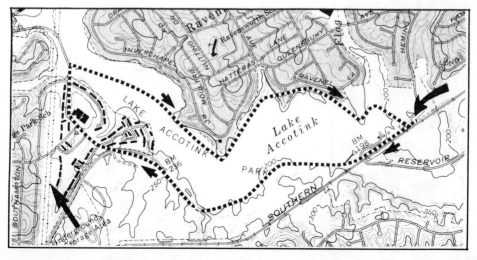

Eakin Community Park

Location: Fairfax County, Virginia, just west of Gallows Road and the Beltway

Distance: 6.5   **Rating**: 2

Surface: Blacktop, gravel, dirt   **Population**: 2

Park in the lot on Prosperity Avenue south of Route 50. Run northwest on the trail across Barkley Avenue existing on Route 50 at Nutley Street which is just west of Covington. Turn at this point and run southeast toward Woodburn Road. When the trail forks southeast of Prosperity Street, run the fork going to the right. Continue southeast and cross Woodburn Road. Run to the right around a field and continue south past King Arthur Road. The trail becomes a small path through the weeds and winds north ending in an old parking lot. Return to your starting point, using the same course.

Special Information: This is an excellent trail at the beginning of the run (about five miles) but it is almost unrunnable south of King Arthur Road. The last one and a half miles of this trail is through tall grass. Eakin Community Park is part of the Fairfax County Park Authority.

Lake Fairfax

Location: Reston, south of Route 606 from Route 7
Distance: 3
Surface: Blacktop, gravel

Rating: 1
Population: 2

Park near the intersection of Route 606 and Lake Fairfax Drive. Run south on Lake Fairfax Drive past the pet farm on the left where you can see exotic animals behind the fence. Run past the gates marking the entrance to the park. Turn right and run down the hill toward the administration building. When you reach the front of the building, continue running south over the spillway from Lake Fairfax. Run up the hill on the road which is blocked at the top and continue running south until you see a sign pointing to an exit. Turn left and follow that sign running east and north down the hill on the side of the road. Follow the road around to Lake Fairfax Drive which will take you back out of the park.

Special Information: In the summer there is an entry fee for non-Fairfax County automobiles. There are picnic areas and campgrounds on the top of the hill in the park. There is even an area marked for cross-country skiing on top of the hill.

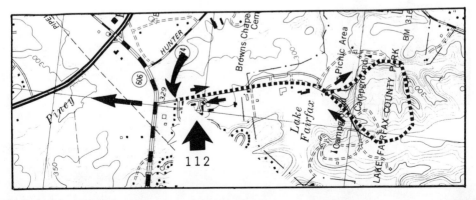

Reston, North Side

Location: Reston, on the Dulles Airport Access Toll Road
Distance: 4.6   **Rating**: 2
Surface: Blacktop, sidewalk   **Population**: 2

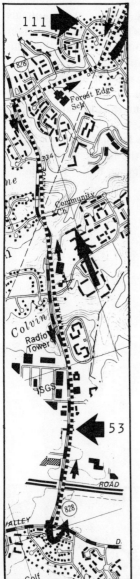

Reston is a planned community with numerous trails. There are more trails on the north side of this community and they are better developed than those in the south.

Park near the northeast corner of Reston and run west from Lake Fairfax Drive on Hunt Club Road. Take the sidewalk on the north side of the road. Cross directly across the center of the circle at King Road emerging on the west side at North Shore Drive, cross over a concrete bridge to the west side of Wiehle Avenue and run south, past Lake Anne. Continue running across Fairfax Drive and North Shore Drive once it loops around. Locate the W&OD Trail before Sunset Hills Road. At the W&OD Trail, return to your starting point.

Special Information: There are numerous runners in the Reston area because of the large number of convenient trails. This trail is over gently rolling terrain.

Reston, Soapstone — South Lakes Trail

Location: Reston, located on the Dulles Airport Access Toll Road
Distance: 2.2   **Rating**: 1
Surface: Blacktop   **Population**: 2

    Start running at the corner of Sunrise Valley and Soapstone Drives. Run south on the east side of the Soapstone Drive until you pick up the trail on the west side (approximately 400 feet). Cross over to the west side running behind some houses and along the golf course. Continue south to South Lakes Drive where a leg of the trail turns west. Run west along the south side of the golf course. In approximately three-quarters of a mile a trail turns north. Turn right onto that trail to run through the center of the golf course. When the trail deadends, turn right to return to the area where you started.

Special Information: Since the west end of this trail passes through a golf course, that segment should only be run when there are not a large number of people on the course.

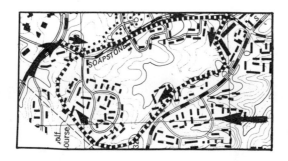

Reston, Southside Wildflower Trail

Location: Reston, located on the Dulles Airport Access Toll Road

Distance: 2.9   **Rating**: 1

Surface: Blacktop   **Population**: 2

   Park off Soapstone Drive and Lawyers Road on the south side of Reston. The trail parallels Lawyers Road in an east/west direction. Run west crossing Steeplechase Drive and locate the split just west of Steeplechase Drive. Take the southern leg and stay to the right making a large circle passing through the Colts Neck Recreation Area. This circle will bring you back to the same split in the trail; this time though you will be approaching from the north. Continue running back to the nature center where you began.

Special Information: There is a horse path which parallels much of this trail. The trail runs behind houses with access to Lawyers Road over land owned by the Reston Home Owners' Association.

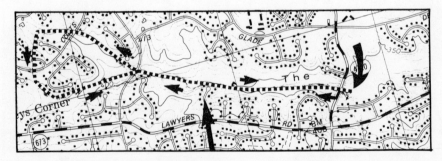

Reston, Westside — USGS

Location: Reston, located on the Dulles Airport Access Toll Road
Distance: 6
Surface: Sidewalk, blacktop, street

Rating: 2
Population: 2

    Start at Reston Avenue, Route 602, just south of the Dulles Access Road. Run south along Reston along the sidewalk on the west side. Turn right on South Lakes Drive and run west along the sidewalk on the south side of the road. Continue west even after the sidewalk stops to the southwest corner of the USGS Drive. Look to the left (south) when you reach this point to find a blacktop trail going into the woods. Run down this trail around a turn and come out on a residential street. Turn right to pick up the trail heading south between houses at the end of the street. Run west behind these houses on a blacktop trail emerging on Glade Drive. Run along the edge of the road for half a block and pick up the trail at the sidewalk on the north side of the street. Run past Dogwood Elementary School around two gentle curves arriving at Freetown Drive half a block before Freetown Drive. Run south along the northwest side of Freetown Drive which will take you in a large circle to the southern end of the street.

Special Information: The USGS is a modern complex. There is still much development underway on this side of Reston. Reston is very runnable and there are many trails through the community. I arbitrarily selected these trails on which to run, but there are many other options available in Reston.

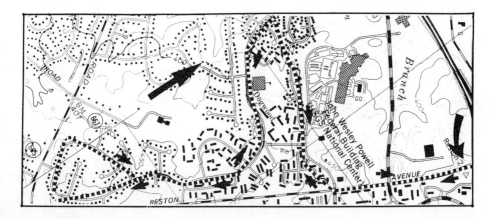

Chapter 10
Washington Area Running Events

The Washington area offers a wide variety of races. From the small *fun runs*, through the 10K races, to full marathons, you can run them all. There are two major marathons in the Washington area. The D.C. Marathon is held in April of every year. It is run in the District of Columbia and covers downtown areas such as Pennsylvania Avenue and quieter areas like Rock Creek Park. The Marine Corps Marathon is held in early November. It is the largest marathon in the area, with approximately 12,000 runners, and most likely the best run in the United States. There is about one Marine providing race-related services for each runner.

Below, I have included 14 of the major Washington area running events. Applications for these races can usually be obtained from local athletic stores one or two months before the event. The Cherry Blossom and Marine Corps Marathons have limitations on the number of entrants due to their extreme popularity. For the avid runner, there are enough other events to keep running almost every weekend of the year.

EVENT

Date	Race
New Year's Day	Ed Barron 10K Hangover Classic
Washington's Birthday	D.C. Roadrunners Washington's Birthday Marathon
1st Saturday in March	Avon 15K (Women Only)
Last of March/ First of April	Cherry Blossom 10 Miler
Mother's Day	Bonnie Bell (Women Only)
3rd Weekend in May	Hometown Run 15K

Date	Race
1st Sunday in June	Hecht's 10 Miler
Last Sunday in August	Annapolis Ten Miler
3rd Saturday in September	Moving Comfort (Women Only)
3rd Saturday of September	Diet Pepsi 10K
September	Masters Championship TAC 30K
1st Sunday in October	D.C. Roadrunner 36 Miler
1st or 2nd Sunday in October	Army Headquarters 10 Miler
1st Weekend in November	Marine Corps Marathon